Pamela Rhatigan

soothe your baby
the natural way

hamlyn

First published in Great Britain in 2005 by Hamlyn,
a division of Octopus Publishing Group Ltd,
2–4 Heron Quays, London E14 4JP

Distributed in the United States and Canada by
Sterling Publishing Co., Inc.
387 Park Avenue South, New York, NY 10016–8810

ISBN 0 600 61175 2
EAN 9780600611752

A CIP catalogue record for this book is available
from the British Library

Printed and bound in China

10 9 8 7 6 5 4 3 2 1

This book is not intended as a substitute for medical advice. The
reader should consult a physician in all matters relating to health.
This book presents a selection of complementary therapies and
techniques that are particularly suitable for babies. However, it must
be stressed that in cases of illness, accidents and other emergencies,
the first and only course of action is to seek help from the family
doctor or emergency services. While the advice and information are
believed to be accurate and true at the time of going to press,
neither the author nor the publisher can accept legal responsibility
or liability for any errors or omissions that may have been made.

contents

introduction

Having a baby is a truly amazing experience, even though we may take it for granted at times. By looking at the many different choices that you have regarding your home, your lifestyle, and that of your loved ones, you can discover effective and empowering techniques that lead to good health, a happy baby and a contented, cared-for family.

Above *The more interaction you have with your baby, the stronger your bonding will be. Don't be afraid to handle your baby. Ask how to support him if you are afraid of being clumsy.*

Looking to your new adventure as a parent, this book will show you how to care for and nurture your child naturally, so that he grows up happily and healthily, in an environment that supports both you and the planet.

Soothe your Baby is filled with effective and empowering ideas to enhance the family environment. By realistically examining what can happen within your relationship and looking at your new responsibilities, we hope this book will evoke ideas that will help both you and your partner in your new roles. It also covers everything you need to know so that you can care in the best possible way for your baby – whether you want to find out about feeding, changing nappies, swaddling, bathing, sleeping, crying or possible illnesses.

natural remedies

This book contains invaluable suggestions to the many common problems that can arise in your child's first years, along with natural remedies for conditions that can be alleviated or prevented. You will find a wealth of information on natural therapies – such as reflexology, homoeopathy, sound therapy, crystal therapy and herbal medicine – that can benefit both you and your baby. You will also be guided on how to massage your baby, which is one of the best things that you can do with your child as it not only aids health and development, but creates a deep, loving and long-lasting attachment.

postive change

No one can ever estimate the amount of change that can occur in your life once you commit to being a parent – in many ways as your baby is born so are you! A whole new world is about to open up for you, full of wonder, amazement and love, as well as responsibility, and mental and physical endurance. Although at times these changes may seem daunting, and you may suffer from feelings of concern or negativity, this book is filled with

Above *Massaging your baby is one of the best ways to promote good health and development, while at the same time fostering a loving bond between you.*

information as to how you can cope with these feelings, and use time-tested therapies and natural non-destructive products to best provide not only for your child but for future generations.

listen to your intuition

Parenting is only as complicated as you make it; listen to your intuition and take your time so that you feel connected to those you love. Don't worry about making sure the house is spotless – concentrate on your baby and spend time bonding, massaging, cuddling and caressing him. Also use this time to bond with your extended family. You will find that older generations can give you great support as well as the benefit of their experience. They can not only give you 'time off' while they look after your baby, but can be good sounding boards if you have any concerns, doubts or problems.

It can also be extremely beneficial to create a new support system for yourself, for example by joining a mother and baby group. It will really help you not only to have other adult contact, but to know that other mothers are in the same situation as you and have the same concerns as you, and that what you are experiencing is completely natural.

hope for the future

Soothe your Baby was born out of my own parenting experiences. My son has been my greatest teacher, and has led me back to natural, intuitive thinking and the age-old medicine of the Earth.

Your baby is now teaching you about love, life and the world, and I hope that my book will guide you to a more natural way of life. Science and technology have moved on enormously in the last hundred years, so use this to your advantage, and help to create a harmonious world where everyone has enough wholesome nutrition and lives in love and peace.

Enjoy your journey.

'Just being born is a miracle, to grow and make a difference in this wonderful world, is grace indeed ... but to live a life that touches others is amazing beyond compare.'

From Tree of Life Inspirations

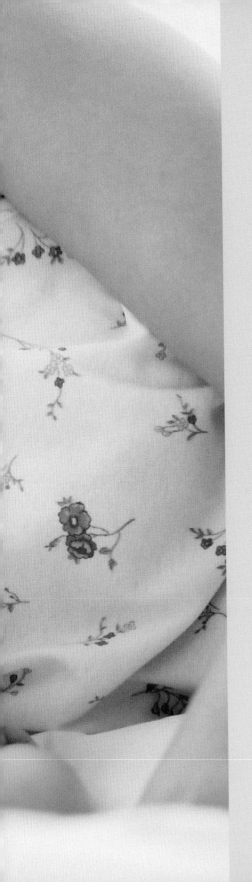

you and your
new arrival

now you're a parent

To look after your baby you will need the patience of a saint, the calmness of a tortoise and the sense of humour of your favourite comedian. There is no training school for the most important job you will ever do, so how do you go about becoming the kind of parent you want your child to have?

***Above** Your baby will be finely tuned into you and how you are feeling. This is part of his survival kit, so how frazzled you are will be reflected in your baby's bahaviour.*

Babies and children can find buttons to push that you never even knew existed. They will demand your attention, and when you are not giving it, they will find an avenue that will usually end in tears. But don't worry, this is all completely normal, and there are ways to cope with it all.

role models

It is a good idea for both parents to sit down and make two lists. First, note all the great qualities you remember and now admire in your own and other parents. Second, make a list of all the things that you never want to repeat with your own child. Compare your lists, think of other things you can add using films, stories or friends for inspiration, and make a new list together so that you can compose an image of your ideal, contented family. That positive imagery is just what you need when your baby lets rip with yet another deafening scream – although make sure that you use this list as a guide and not a rule book.

quality time

The more quality time you can give to your baby, the better. Babies are babies for such a short time, and this time can never be repeated. So if the house is a mess and chores don't get done, you probably have a happy, satisfied and contented baby.

It is also vitally important that you keep up a good dialogue with your partner. You are both going through emotional upheaval and your relationship can be expected to undergo major changes, so you need to be aware of how the other is coping. Simply listening can be as useful as giving out advice. You will find that your main topic of conversation now revolves around what your baby is doing, and the tiniest bit of change can occupy your whole evening. This kind of dialogue allows you to share the experiences of being a parent, and can help a partner working during the day to feel more involved.

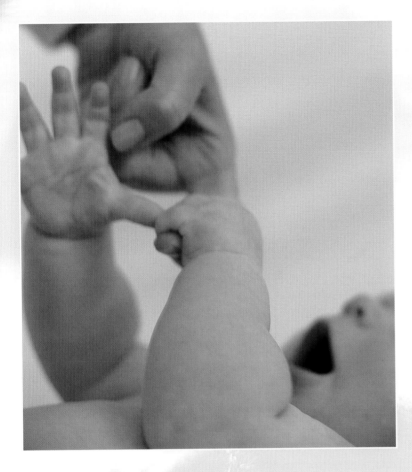

focus on the positive

Every stage your baby goes through is transitory, so it is essential that you make the most of it. Any bad experiences you may have as a parent can often overshadow the good times, even when there are substantially more good times than bad. So train your mind to focus on the positive and learn to laugh at the dramas.

Your positive input is also invaluable to your child, so make sure you laugh, nurture and pamper your baby. It will affect her self-perception, confidence and emotional security for the rest of her life. When you are finding it hard to cope, focus on the times when your baby makes you feel full of love, joy and contentment, and keep that alive in your heart. Your baby can sense your emotions, so if she feels your love and positive vibes she will be happier and more content because of it. There will be emotionally rough times to cope with, but these will be more than balanced by exquisite experiences.

COPING WITH CHANGE

The challenges you will face are not just physical, like the effort of having to drag yourself out of bed yet again. Ideas that just don't work, bringing frustration and even anger, can make you feel helpless. Your emotional development is about to go up a level as you learn how to deal rationally and cope with these strange feelings. Remember, a kind word, gentle touch and smiling eyes can change how a person feels.

bonding

Bonding with your baby is not necessarily as easy or instinctive as it was once thought to be. If you don't feel an instantaneous, rapturous surge of love when the baby is first handed to you, don't worry, the bonding process can take time, and there are simple ways to encourage it.

***Above** Hold your baby's face close to yours so that she can easily start to focus on you, making out your features and seeing your smiling face and shining, happy eyes.*

Some women feel a bond with their baby immediately after the birth, some will feel it after a couple of days, while others may not feel it for a couple of years or even at all. Mothers are usually helped naturally by their body's chemicals and hormones, since during and straight after birth high levels of endorphins are released to both mother and baby. These encourage feelings of euphoria and elation, and the effects of these natural opiates create a state of inter-dependency that in turn allows attachment to develop. However, you will find that the more you stimulate a baby, the more response you will get, which can help to connect mother with child. So take your time to get to know this little stranger, using touch, stroking, humming or singing, baby chatter and facial expressions. Boys are likely to be more active and want to touch everything, whereas girls prefer the human face and visual stimulation, so they may be more attentive to your expresssions.

Bonding does not mean that you have to feel love gushing out of you constantly. Feelings of protectiveness are signs of bonding and they stimulate nurturing and caring reactions.

connecting through the eyes

Your newborn baby can be very alert, and will stare intently. A newborn can focus to about 20–25 cm (8–10 in), but bright light will make him want to close his eyes. Once you are able to soften the lights or close the curtains, you can then begin to explore each other's faces and eyes. Let your baby slowly focus on your smiling face, holding him at a distance of about 20 cm (8 in). Looking into your baby's eyes can initiate engulfing waves of love.

bonding through touch

In the womb babies receive all their information from sensory input, through the skin and the whole of their back, which is in contact with the mother's uterus. In their new, changed environment, touch is vital. In native cultures babies are gently stroked from the minute of their birth, lying on top of

Left Gently stroking or kissing can de-stress your baby and make you feel very protective.

their mother's stomach. Most babies enjoy the sensation of being stroked, touched and massaged (see pages 80–101), which can be very reassuring.

bonding through sound

Your baby was aware of external sounds while in the womb, such as music, television and, most importantly, voices, albeit muffled. He is used to hearing your voice, and the voices of the rest of the family, and recognizes these familiar sounds as reassuring, so softly and quietly talk, hum, sing or chant to your baby. As you sing let your hands softly and rhythmically pat or stroke your baby's body. Play music that you enjoy listening to and happiness hormones will be released into your body, relaxing you. Dance with your baby held close to you. The sounds will vibrate though both your bodies and can ease any tension, allowing a joining to take place between you. A sense of union can be discovered through your soft tones.

feeding

The hormone responsible for bringing in the mother's milk also plays a part in stimulating maternal instincts, and breastfeeding creates an opportunity for closeness. In this position your baby can see your smiling face, hear your cooing voice and smell you. If you are bottle-feeding, try to do so in a similar position to breastfeeding, in order to achieve the same closeness. You could try bottle-feeding your baby with no layers of clothing between you to simulate the closeness of breast-feeding.

BONDING WITH PREMATURE BABIES

If your baby is in an incubator, whatever physical contact you can have will be of benefit to you both. If possible try to stroke your baby or place your hand on him and send love from your heart through your fingertips. Your voice will be important to your baby and has the potential to be very healing. Humming vibrates cells, molecules, organs and the whole body. You could hum a tune, a continuous note or a succession of notes, and your baby will hear and absorb the loving concern in your voice.

Sound and touch are effective ways of coping with physical separation. You will be reassuring your baby and calming him with your presence and touch, and you will feel more positive and strong knowing that you are doing something to help to build a connection between you both.

being a family

This wonderful, helpless bundle is going to claim a lot of your time and love, which is great, as long as you don't forget the rest of the family and their needs. Every member can add to the harmony in the home, but they must feel nourished so that they can voluntarily add their own contribution.

Above *Family life, like everything else, is something we acquire gradually rather than overnight.*

realistic expectations

As a new family you are full of expectations of your life together. How attached you are to these expectations dictates the amount of disappointment you feel if things do not go strictly to plan. It is important to realize that you cannot map out your life to the letter. You can have ideals and make plans, but you must be able and willing to adapt those plans to fit in with any changes in your circumstances. Learn to accept life's new turns, to work with them. Don't resist change or stick to the old ways that can become useless and redundant as your life moves on. Being a family is an emotional, physical, mental and spiritual learning curve.

grandparents

If your baby has grandparents who want to be involved, then this should benefit all, and strengthen the family unit. Grandparents usually love to be useful (but not used), and have a lot of knowledge to offer. They can also take the pressure off you when you are tired. In order to maintain a positive relationship with your parents, listen to their advice (even though you don't always have to adhere to it) and in turn, share your ideas with them. Sometimes this is a chance for them to make up for their own mistakes, so welcome your parents and try to resolve any tensions between you. Your baby will probably be doted on, growing in confidence due to all that love.

jealousy

Jealousy is destructive, and a jealous sibling or partner needs reassurance. When it seems that all your attention is being given to the baby, insecurities arise and can even change into resentment. To stop jealous tendencies arising, try to involve all the members of the family in the care of a new infant and the decisions that are being made. Don't make too much fuss over little things, or demand that things are always done your way.

Above Sibling rivalry can be a problem after the birth of a new baby, but if you involve your older child in caring for the new arrival, this may ease some of the tensions.

siblings – bonding for brothers and sisters

A new baby can put an older sibling's nose considerably out of joint. As a mother you are busy with the new baby and more tired and fraught than you previously were. Until recently, your older children were the focus of all your attention, but now, for the first time, they have to learn to share you. Helping your child to bond with the new baby and showing them that you still love them can successfully alleviate the problems of sibling rivalry.

First of all, when the new baby cries let the older child know that it is because she is frightened, not because she doesn't like him.

The more helpful and protective a sibling feels towards his new brother or sister, the less likely that he will be affected by sibling rivalry. So it is important that you include him in as many aspects of the baby's care as possible. If they want to, encourage the sibling to talk to and help out with the new baby, and praise them when they do. Let him choose how to dress his little brother or sister. Let him sit in a safe, comfortable chair and cuddle the baby, or ask him to draw pictures or take photographs of the baby to send to family and friends. Ask your older child for ideas on how to calm and comfort the baby, offering praise if it works and promising to try it again another time if it doesn't. Finally, if they are able to, let the oldest help around the house. This may lead to more work, but will make your child feel important and useful.

you are still special

To ensure that your oldest child does not feel left out at the birth of his new sibling, give him a present or privilege to celebrate the arrival of the baby. Let him know that the new baby loves him too.

Remember to keep reassuring your child that you are always going to be there for him, and back this up with lots of cuddles and kisses. Make sure you spend quality time alone with your first-born, doing something that he enjoys. Tell him that he is special and you love him. Let him know that you are feeling more tired then usual and perhaps have a cuddly afternoon nap with him.

NATURAL REMEDIES

If your oldest remains jealous, try homeopathy, Bach flower remedies, let him choose a small tumbled crystal, or place one in his bedroom.

you and your partner

It is very easy for you and your partner to become so focussed on your new baby that you ignore the needs of each other. It is important that the two of you not only spend quality time enjoying each other's company, but that each partner also gets time to themselves so they can relax, even if it is just for ten minutes.

Above *Make time for your partner when you can cuddle and connect in order to keep your partnership vital and loving.*

remember each other

It is all too easy to get lost in the rapture of new love and forget your partner, so do spend time together, not doing chores but cuddling and connecting with a feeling of oneness. Remember to laugh, to hug, to say sorry, be silly, play childishly, to be flexible and to make compromises. Take the time to tell your partner that you appreciate them and what they are doing and that you love them. Make the effort to make each other happy. You will both appreciate it and it will also have a positive effect on your baby who will sense this loving atmosphere.

personal space

You and your partner will have lost your personal space for a while, and you both need to reclaim a little of it if you are to remain contented with family life and with each other. You occasionally need to be able to recharge your batteries and to retreat from everyday life and its problems. So allow each other to take complete charge of the baby while the other enjoys a long, luxurious bath, reads a book, potters in the garden or simply watches a favourite television programme.

how fathers can help

As well as helping with the practicalities of looking after a new baby and bonding with her, a new father will need to be aware of the needs of his partner, both actual and emotional (as will the new mother). One of the things a mother wants from her partner at this time is for him to do some of the chores she used to do, such as food shopping, laundry and general tidying.

Sympathy and understanding, empathy and tolerance are also greatly appreciated. A father's support can make all the difference to a mother's earliest experience of parenthood. If possible, a father should give his partner the time she needs to bond with her baby and provide that child's nutritional needs, while reassuring her she is doing a good job.

neediness

Often we expect our partners to be mind readers, and if they don't respond to our undisclosed needs, our demands can push them further away. The more you need something, the more it controls everything you do, and the less likely you are to get this requirement met. If you keep your feelings bottled up, and subsequently they are never met, your baby may become the focus of your unfulfilled dreams, and pouring misplaced love in her direction can create a particularly demanding child. So it is important to discuss what it is you are relying on in one another to supply within your emotional, mental and physical lives. You will often find that once you have spoken about these needs, they will cease to have a hold over you.

romantic lovemaking resumes

Hormones play a leading part in sexual arousal for both men and women. The new mother's hormones are in the middle of a major readjustment. Gone, for a while at least, are the moments of lustful indulgence, but they can be replaced with more meaningful moments of true togetherness and a connection at a much deeper level, where you truly feel close, content and totally united with just a hug. Fulfilling, pleasurable sex is temporarily replaced by loving caresses that will reawaken the desires in time. Try sexual massage in preparation for the resumption of lovemaking, a gentle style of teasing the body awake.

LOVERS SPEAK WITHOUT WORDS

This is such a special and short time, so make the most of it. Be tolerant of mess and untidiness, generate feelings of blissful love and snuggle up together, allowing warmth and tenderness to seep through you.

There will be times when you just want to be together, so don't answer the telephone or door; this is your special time, so make the most of it.

Treat yourselves to a relaxing foot massage by each sitting at the end of a sofa or bed, gently and fondly massaging each other's feet, then spend some time simply cuddling each other.

the father's role

Fathers can be inadvertently overlooked when a new baby joins the family. The life that they have been used to is about to change dramatically, and fathers are usually expected to just adapt immediately and get on with it. They may often feel that their partner is the one getting all the support and attention.

Above *Babies are not necessarily as solid as one expects them to be, and you will find they wriggle a lot. However, the more you play with them, the more confident you will become.*

a father's feelings

A new father can be just as overwhelmed with a wealth of emotions or concerns as a new mother. Some men see their role as that of protector, and feel pressurized by burdening financial concerns. For others, unknown emotions will surface, and for some there is even disappointment at the gender of the child, an emotion that many do not want to admit to. A father can experience unexpected feelings of loss, as his partner totally focuses on the baby's needs. In the first few months feelings of rejection, jealousy and loneliness are common. Men cannot explain why they feel usurped by this fragile little bundle that you had both been so looking forward to; or they feel so much love that they think they will burst open. A father may be looking forward to sharing the experiences he enjoyed as a child with his own father, such as camping or fishing. He will have his own ideals of how a father should behave, but because of tiredness, anxiety, never-ending washing and relentless crying – from the baby that is – this is not the behaviour he exhibits. On top of all this the father is still expected to be calm, understanding and sympathetic.

talking it through

Some men still do not speak readily about their fears and worries, either because it's not in their nature, they fear it's not manly or they worry that they will be seen as unable to cope. A new baby brings about a huge change in everyone's life and open communication is imperative. If resentment becomes an issue, marriages or partnerships can founder in that first year of a baby's life, so always talk things through.

Just as it is important for mothers to meet up and share experiences, it is also a good idea for fathers to do the same. In postnatal groups, fathers can be reassured by learning that other men are in the same situations and going through similar ordeals, and they can find out how they can deal with the same daunting problems.

handling and talking to baby

A father should be encouraged to make physical contact with his child, and not just through chores like changing nappies. Cuddling and holding baby close allows both father and child to get to know each other's smell, and scent is a strong motivator for attachment.

Your baby will have heard her father's voice while in the womb, and will be comforted by it now. A father and baby can feel connected through simple communication, and a special baby language, spoken in a lowered and softened voice, creates a very personal bond.

share the care

Fathers need to feel involved with all aspects of parenting, and this can also help them to bond with their baby, so it is important that the father shares as much of the care as possible. If he is around and helping, especially during the early, formative stages, he will easily tune into his baby's needs, her cries and her love, creating a strong father–child bond that encourages happy, confident children, and can help the father deal with his changing needs and emotions.

Fathers are now more involved than ever before, from the onset of pregnancy to being present at the birth (about 90 per cent attend the birth), and an ever-growing number of men are staying at home to look after the children while the mother returns to work. As a consequence men are learning the joy of being the primary care-giver and all the benefits that entails.

STAYING CLOSE

One of the best ways for a father to get physically close to his new baby is by carrying her in a sling. This is a very comforting way to carry a baby because she can feel her parent's heartbeat in close proximity and can enjoy the natural movement of the parent.

There are a wide variety of slings to choose from, and most can be used from the outset. However, if the mother has back pain after giving birth she may not be able to use a sling, making it all the more useful if the father can.

feeling low

Baby blues and postnatal depression are phrases that are often heard and you may worry that you are suffering from them. However, because of a host of changing hormonal, physical and logistical circumstances, new mothers may just be experiencing more general emotional lows than their partners rather than depression.

Above *Try to spend as much time as you can outside. If you don't have a garden, you could take your baby to a local park with a friend.*

causes

There are a number of reasons why you may be feeling low. After childbirth the hormones associated with being pregnant and giving birth start trying to return to a more balanced state, which could cause you some emotional turmoil. Coupled with this, the huge, frightening responsibility of caring for a new baby can cause a drained and tired mother to become totally overwhelmed by the new situation she is in.

You may also be missing a social life and the company of other adults, for example, friends from your workplace; worrying about having to return to work and who will care for your child; or have concerns about how your relationship with your partner is faring.

breastfeeding problems

Mothers who find it difficult to breastfeed can become anxious and feel as if they are failing. If you cannot relax while trying to breastfeed, your milk may be less nutritionally satisfying, leaving your baby unfulfilled, which in turn can make you feel inadequate. A caesarean delivery or traumatic birth may make moving around and holding your newborn very uncomfortable or even painful, which does nothing for your overall state of mind.

lack of self-esteem

Finding that you still have a large tummy, that appears to have absolutely no muscle tone left, and the thought that you may never look good or appealing again, can create great sadness and a misplaced fear of losing your partner's love.

After having a baby many people feel lonely within their marriage, which can exacerbate any low feelings you may be experiencing. Talking and willingly making time for each other is therefore of the utmost importance. Discuss what it is that makes you feel wanted and needed, so that you can give this to each other regularly.

Left Going for a walk is a good way to spend time together as a family, and exercise is a great tonic if you are feeling low.

sleep deprivation

We cannot underestimate the effect that lack of sleep has on any human being. At this time, you and your partner will both be wearier than you have ever been in your lives. You are likely to snap at each other, and grievances kept in a cerebral storeroom will eventually surface, blown out of all proportion.

To try and mimimize the effects of sleep deprivation make sure that you sleep whenever you can, and accept any help that friends or relatives may offer so that you have fewer chores to do and can have a nap when your baby is sleeping, without worrying about how much you need to do.

baby blues and postnatal depression

During the first week after giving birth it is normal to feel emotional and irrational, irritable and touchy, depressed and anxious and likely to burst into tears. This emotional rollercoaster is known as the 'baby blues'.

Postnatal depression, on the other hand, usually occurs ten to fourteen weeks after delivery, although it can appear any time in the first year. It can be difficult to diagnose because the symptoms are so varied, and very similar to those usually associated with feeling low after childbirth. They include insomnia; wanting to sleep excessively; increase or loss of appetite; uncontrollable crying; lethargy; feeling unable to cope; feeling guilty, inadequate and worthless; claustrophobia; thinking that you are mentally unstable with suicidal and baby-harming thoughts – very rarely actioned; loss of concentration; anxiety and panic attacks; and loss of interest in your baby.

Postnatal depression is a medical condition and if you think you have it you must seek help. Total loving support from those around you, combined with exercise and the nutritional advice listed on page 23 will help in conjunction with the advice of a professional.

POSTNATAL DEPRESSION IN MEN

Postnatal depression in men is often not recognized or treated, either by the father himself or the medical profession. The main focus of attention is on the well-being of the new arrival and mother – the new father may not want to speak up, and in so doing cause more problems. There is no shame and should never be any embarrassment on the father's part if he feels that some of the symptoms listed opposite affect him. Medical advice should be sought, and the help provided by a doctor can be accompanied by a good mood-enhancing diet (see page 23).

boosting your mood

Babies can sense stress and unrest, but cannot possibly understand what it all means. This causes them to be cranky and demanding, which just makes everything worse for the already tense parent. So it stands to reason that the more contented you are, the better it is for everyone. Soothing yourself goes a long way to soothing your baby.

CLEARING THE AIR, LITERALLY

After a heated discussion you can sometimes still feel the tension around you, so it is therapeutic to "clear the air". A good way to do this is to open the windows and let the fresh air in. You can also put fresh flowers in the room, light a candle or use either American sage, incense or natural essence sprays. Sea salt in a glass container will also absorb negativity, but should be discarded after a few days.

ways to boost your mood

There are a number of ways that you can boost your mood, such as ensuring that you get enough sunlight; by regular exercise such as walking, swimming or yoga; eating a good, balanced diet; and having contact with other parents.

benefits of sunlight

Vitamin D is formed naturally when the skin is exposed to sunlight, and sunlight also boosts energizing, mood-enhancing hormones that are being negatively affected by low oestrogen, so go for a walk in the daylight, even if it is overcast. The exertion of walking for just ten minutes will release feel-good hormones into your bloodstream. As this becomes a regular routine, your metabolism will also speed up, helping you to lose gained weight.

the importance of a good diet

Rest and good food aid the recovery and build-up of depleted energy, so eat a varied diet, rich in fruit and vegetables (preferably organic) but low in saturated fats, sugar and caffeine. You will need some carbohydrates for energy, but avoid processed food and refined white bread and choose wholemeal or wholegrain. Avoid fried food and eat good sources of protein such as quinoa, brown rice, fish, chicken, eggs and beans. Snack on seeds, nuts, oatcakes, rice cakes and fruit and use honey instead of sugar. You have transferred a large supply of zinc to your baby, so to replace it eat nuts, wholegrains, oats and lentils. Zinc needs vitamin B6 in particular to work, so also supplement with a vitamin B complex.

breastfeeding alternatives

If you are having difficulties breastfeeding, see your midwife, health-visitor or breast-feeding counsellor. You could also ask your partner to feed your baby with a bottle. If you need a rest or are becoming tired, express your milk and then bottle feed this to your baby.

Above Try to find other parents in your area. There are many groups around that will link you up with others going through similar experiences to you.

don't shelve your problems

When problems get stored away they breed resentment, so always deal with problems as they arise. If your temper does not allow for a mature conversation, have a strategy in place that gives you both some breathing space in order to calm down. Then try to discuss the problem again, calmly and quietly. Try not to blame one another and always let each other know how this problem is making you feel.

Remember that all human beings have failings, and when you love someone you overlook these traits – although at times this can be hard to do. Neither of you are experts in this field – who is? You are going through a learning process together, and need to share your experiences and thoughts on it, even if you think your partner might not agree with you.

meet other parents

Women who have given up work may now feel especially lonely and miss the workplace camaraderie. This is exactly the time you need to be talking to other parents, to discover that you are all going through the same experiences. So join local mother-and-baby groups or baby massage classes.

FOODS TO BOOST YOUR MOOD

- Oily fish
- Turkey
- Soya
- Beans
- Seeds
- Milk
- Wholegrain bread
- Green vegetables
- Sweet peppers
- Carrots
- Garlic
- Apples
- Apricots
- Bananas
- Lime

BENEFICIAL SUPPLEMENTS

- Vitamin B complex
- Vitamin C
- Iron
- Magnesium
- Zinc
- Evening primrose

choosing the natural way

Choosing the natural way involves taking time to make yourself aware of what the products you buy contain, and using plant- or energy-based therapies to maintain good health. This lifestyle is about buying organic, reusable and bio-degradable products where possible, including clothes, furniture, bedding, paints and household cleaners.

To be termed natural, a product need only contain small amounts of natural ingredients, and can even be from genetically-modified sources. You can only do what you think is best with the information you are given, so make sure you have as much information as possible. Read the product's label, which lists the ingredients and often tells you what the packaging is made from. There are also websites and magazines – available from newsagents and health-food shops – that can help you make informed choices by advising you on the harmful chemicals that some products contain.

There are a few simple changes that you can make from the outset.

Above *Try to prepare organic food for your baby – and eat organic food yourself when you are breastfeeding.*

eat organic

Food allergies and intolerances that may trigger eczema and asthma can be caused by the chemicals used during the food's growth and processing. So if you are breastfeeding you should eat organic foods, and when you start to wean your baby make sure you do so on organic vegetables and fruit. Organic food has been grown in chemical-free soil and is not from a genetically-modified source.

bottles

Make sure the plastic feeding bottles you buy are not made from polycarbonate, which contains bisphenol A, a hormone-disrupting chemical that can seep into the milk inside. Look on the packaging for PC 7, which indicates the presence of polycarbonate, or for the number 7 inside the recycling triangle.

nappies

A disposable nappy takes hundreds of years to decompose in a landfill site. This in turn damages the environment and our ongoing food chain. However it is not only the environment that benefits from your use of

Left Natural fabrics are comfortable for your baby and can minimize skin irritations.

reusable nappies. For your baby these cotton nappies are soft and comfortable and they also do not contain any chemical gels. The cotton fibres facilitate air circulation, so the skin can keep cool and breathe easily and the nappies do not cause discomfort by rubbing or leaking. Moreover, they do not take any longer to put on.

Natural cotton nappies are also cheaper to use than disposable nappies, even taking into consideration the detergent and electricity used to wash them. There are companies that supply, collect and wash reusable nappies, bringing a fresh supply every week. You can check that they use an environmentally friendly detergent before you sign up.

artificial scent

Fragranced means synthetically perfumed, and one scent can contain 40–50 ingredients, many of which are toxic chemicals. So buy household soaps that don't contain synthetic fragrances and open a window rather than using an air freshener.

Our skin is our largest organ and absorbs as much as 60 per cent of whatever is applied to it. Babies have a larger area of surface skin to weight than adults, meaning that what they absorb is more concentrated. With this in mind, bubble baths, body lotions and sunscreens for babies should also be checked for chemicals and colourants. Whenever possible, choose organic, natural skin-care products.

KEEPING IT NATURAL IN THE HOME

Look around the house and garden to decide if there are any changes you can make to benefit the well-being of the whole family.

- Always turn off computers and televisions when not in use because electrical fields from computers, televisions, lights and microwaves affect our brainwaves, which can lead to mood changes.
- Most easy-care polycotton or crease-resistant bedding is treated with chemicals, so choose the natural, cotton option.
- Carpets can be backed with PVC that gives off a gas, and they trap dust and chemicals that can aggravate asthma and eczema. Can you choose wooden floors or tiles instead?
- Avoid using paint or varnish with high VOC – volatile organic chemicals – levels, which can irritate the lungs. Some are also carcinogenic and contribute to climate change. As an alternative use water-based products.
- MDF usually contains formaldehyde glue, so choose real wood.
- Avoid using pesticides.
- Avoid using products coated with creosote.

caring for your baby

your baby's needs

Your baby needs to feel loved, nurtured, cared for and connected to you. He wants to feel as secure in the outside world as he did in your womb, so it is important to create a warm, loving space at home. Your baby needs to be absolutely sure that you are there for him, because if you are not he will become confused and afraid.

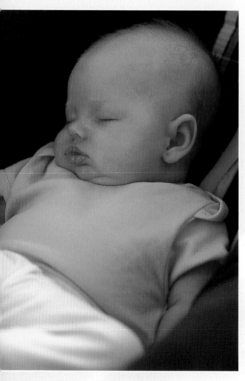

Above Your newborn baby will sleep for as much as 18 hours a day and it can take several months for him to distinguish between night and day.

As well as making sure that your baby is well fed, warm, safe and reassured, there are ways that you can minimize any health risks. These include having good personal hygiene so you do not expose your baby to too many germs, and not smoking around your child or in the home.

sleeping

To begin with your baby will probably sleep for around 16–17 hours a day, dropping to 13–14 hours by the time he is six months old. As he gets older, your baby's sleeping patterns will become more regular. By six months your child will probably start to be sleeping through the night, with two naps during the day. (See also page 48.)

feeding

Until about six months old, milk supplies all the nutrients that a baby needs. Once you begin to introduce solid foods milk still remains an important part of his diet (see page 54). You can continue to breastfeed for as long as you feel comfortable doing so. (See also page 52).

crying

The only way that your baby has to communicate his needs and get them attended to is to cry for your help and loving reassurance. Crying is a survival tactic for a baby, and it is not until they are older that they learn to use tears as a way to get attention. (See also pages 32–5.)

warmth and protection

It is very important that your baby is kept warm – but isn't too hot – as he has an immature thermal system and cannot regulate his own body temperature (see also page 31). You also need to be aware of what your baby's body temperature should be so that you can detect if he has a fever, which may indicate illness. (See also page 33).

Left *Breast milk supplies a newborn baby with all the nutrients he needs.*

It is also very important that you are scrupulous about your own hygiene, washing your hands regularly, and that your baby is kept clean (although this doesn't mean that you need to bath him every day [see pages 40–43]). You also need to try to ensure that he does not come into contact with infectious diseases. However, don't be too obsessive as your baby does need certain exposure to bugs so that his immune system can develop.

loving touch

Your newborn can be comforted by any means of skin-to-skin handling, such as cuddling or caressing, and massage can be especially soothing (see pages 80–83). Embracing your baby while you are both naked, for example, when in bed or the bath, is also very comforting for him.

However, there are some babies who do not like to be handled. A baby who is not comfortable being cuddled will stiffen his body and cry when you hold him, which can be very difficult to cope with.

HIGH-NEED BABIES

High-need babies require lots of attention and are very demanding on both parents. They never want to be away from a parent, are unable to settle and are constantly fretting. They often want to be on the breast, but don't always feed. They want to sleep, but cry instead. They are uneasy with strangers, startle easily and often arch away from you. This type of behaviour can make high-need babies difficult to bond with since they don't seem to be responsive to your efforts to comfort and nurture, and are exhausting.

High-need babies will take longer to adapt to life outside the warmth and safety of the womb. The parents' feelings may get overstretched with the constant fickleness and often unattainable connection, but try not to let that get in the way of loving him. The more you respond rapidly and lovingly, the quicker he will settle. La Leche is an organization set up to help mothers with high-need babies.

your premature baby

A premature baby looks so very tiny and helpless that it is often difficult for a parent to know how to care for them, so seek all the professional help that is available. But there are many ways that parents of premature babies can be helped to bond with their babies.

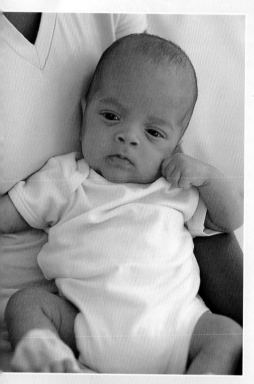

Above *The stomachs of premature (and newborn) babies can hold only a very small amount of milk, so after feeding they are often sick and will then cry as they are hungry again.*

Parents of premature babies need a lot of reassurance, and should get all the professional advice they can. Talking to midwives, hospital counsellors and breastfeeding advisors can help dramatically in this situation. For the parents, one of the most difficult aspects of having a premature baby is that they are unable to hold her and may feel that they cannot bond. However, there are ways to get around this.

feeding

Many full-term babies take up to 48 hours to fully get to grips with suckling, and preterm babies will often take longer. The rooting reflex is necessary for babies to find their source of food, but in a premature baby this reflex can be underdeveloped, so feeding needs extra time and possibly help. The breastfeeding advisor at the hospital will be able to give you good advice on feeding. If possible, try laying your baby alongside you, belly to belly, nose to nipple, and bringing your baby to your breast or bottle. Babies who are tube fed can be simultaneously breastfed, or have your expressed milk fed to them by a tube.

skin and touch

Premature babies have very sensitive skin. By watching their response to being stroked you will be able to gauge how much they can take. Signs of distress, apart from crying, can be muscle spasms, irregular breathing, skin colour change, sneezing and flailing arms. The touch must be smooth, slow and long, a loving caress. In many cases it is better to just rest your hand in one place on her body, and imagine your hand spreading out to encompass her whole body. Some premature babies might prefer skin-to-skin cuddling. You do not have to hold her for this, she could just be lying on top of you, her chest on yours or across your belly.

If your baby is in an incubator and you cannot hold her, you can still talk softly to her, touch her gently and have your milk fed to her through a tube.

swaddling

Some babies feel very insecure in this new world, and freedom of movement may be a contributing factor. Inside the womb they had restricted movements, now they don't. Wrapping your baby in a shawl or soft blanket can help to give her the sensation of being in that controlling safe space again, which in turn makes her feel secure.

how to swaddle

Fold a muslin (in summer) or soft cotton sheet into a triangle and lay your baby gently in the middle. Fold one corner across and tuck it under her back, reasonably tight. Fold the other corner over likewise. Some babies will prefer to have their arms outside. Tuck the remaining corner over the feet. Do not wrap your baby up so tight that she is unable to move, which would not induce sleep or relaxation; or make the swaddle loose enough to be kicked off. The idea is for your baby to feel held, not squeezed.

Never cover your baby's head since this can lead to overheating. Babies need to move around and especially need to move their hands as they lose heat through their head and their hands. Remember that a baby does not have the ability to monitor her own termperature control, so check that she is not obstructed by other bedding. Your baby should always sleep on her back with her feet at the base of the cot.

when to swaddle

A baby can be swaddled whenever she seems unsettled. There is scientific evidence to show that this age-old custom gives your newborn baby a better, more comforting, restful and health-promoting sleep. In fact, in many cultures babies are constantly swaddled.

Once swaddled, your baby can easily be attached to your body, allowing you to have your hands free so you can continue with your everyday routine. As your baby now has the rhythmical motion of your body's movements, she will feel safe and will often be lulled to sleep.

A baby who cries when you put her in her cot, but stops as soon as you lift her up, will benefit from swaddling. She obviously craves some contact, and swaddling could give her the security of something touching her that she needs in order to settle.

If your baby is fidgety when feeding, swaddling her will restrict her movement so that she concentrate on feeding more.

Above *Tiny babies are easier to hold when swaddled, plus they feel more secure and contained as the swaddling recreates the feeling of security they had in the womb.*

crying

When babies cry they are sending out a clear signal for help, and are teaching you to develop your intuition. It can be very frightening to hear, but remember that at this time crying is entirely natural – and is in fact the only way your baby knows how to communicate his needs with you.

Above *Crying is the only way your baby has to let you know that something is amiss – he may be hungry, cold, wet, or just simply lonely.*

Sometimes you will be able to read his lament and soothe him immediately. At other times you will try everything to absolutely no avail. You are not a bad parent for feeling frustrated and angry when your baby cannot be pacified. Every parent goes through a breaking point.

attending to the tears

If not attended to, your baby will either get totally disheartened, and give up, feeling miserable and alone, or increase the volume and intensity to fever pitch. Emotional development is being affected even now, if no-one answers his calls he will eventually withdraw into himself; if someone does, he feels confident and safe again.

Attending to your baby's cry promptly allows you to observe the signals that may indicate what it is that he needs. Parents soon learn to understand if babies are hungry, tired, bored or overstimulated. Let your intuition take over and you will find that your trust and confidence in yourself will increase as you start to realize what your baby wants.

causes for tears

As well as when hungry, wet or tired, babies cry to indicate all manner of experiences. Babies often cry when being dressed or bathed, because they don't feel safe and their skin doesn't like the air.

If you have tried to alleviate the cries in all the usual ways – feeding, nappy changing, rocking for sleep – place your fingers on the back of your baby's neck to check his temperature. You may simply need to add or remove some layers of clothing.

Overstimulated babies will fidget and cry, even though they are extremely tired. Some babies will respond more to a visual stimuli, others to a sound, so try to work out which is predominant for your baby. For example, a hanging mobile will do more to keep a visually stimulated baby awake, than to send them off to sleep.

coping with the crying

When your baby cries, sometimes you will be able to identify the cause of their sobbing and fix the problem, at other times an action that did the trick before does not help in the least. You may find that you have tried everything in your arsenal with absolutely no results, and you will feel like just walking away from it all, or even being angry with your child. As long as your frustration does not lead to physical harm, and you don't show your anger, just remember that these feelings are quite normal and that you are not a bad parent. In this situation one of the best things you can do is ask for help. Phone a relative or friend, or if you have no one to turn to there are helplines you can call. If that person can come and take over for five minutes or a few hours, it will allow you time to gather your thoughts and refresh your mind. If practical help is not an option, then simply talking to someone can have a tremendously positive effect on your attitude. You need to be reassured that you are not failing yourself or your baby, and to understand that other parents go through exactly the same tough times.

When inside the womb, your baby was affected by your state, since the hormones you released entered your baby through the placenta. If you can remember what you did to soothe yourself when you were pregnant, such as listening to a certain piece of music or moving your body in a certain way, try repeating that together, as your baby has an imprint of this being calming.

TESTING YOUR BABY'S TEMPERATURE

Your child's normal body temperature should be between 36°C and 37°C (96.8°F to 98.6°F). Higher temperatures than this may indicate a fever and you should call your doctor.

If you do not have access to a thermometer, use the back of your hand on the back of your baby's neck or tummy – if you were in a panic your palm would begin to sweat, so would not give you accurate feedback.

Shivers, tremors and trembles can mean overheating, not that your baby is cold. To wrap him up more, would be dangerous for him. Babies should not be sweaty, so remove layers if this is the case.

recognizing your child's different cries

As you become more attuned to your baby's needs and learn to trust your intuition, you will soon be able to recognize the following cries.

Above *There are telephone help lines available for distraught parents, that can help to calm your fears when your baby cannot be pacified and may be driving you to distraction.*

the whimper

A bored, low-pitched cry indicates a general sense of being uncomfortable, perhaps because she has wind, needs to move or because the lights are too bright. Try a gentle rock, patting the back or humming a soft, soothing tone.

attention cry

A sudden loud cry that gets louder indicates that your baby wants your attention. Try to rock her in position with your hands, and talk in a gentle, soft voice. If this does not work check her temperature and nappy and try keeping her with you for a snuggle.

A baby that is only cuddled or gets a reaction when she cries soon learns that this is the best or only way to get you to focus on her. You can counteract this reaction by ensuring that you give her plenty of attention all the time, not just when she cries. If you cuddle her, play with her, talk to her, sing to her, and involve her in whatever you are doing – including housework and other everyday chores – she won't need to cry for you.

tired cry

This long, wailing sound is accompanied by fidgeting, head movements and the rubbing of eyes. Try to rock her off to sleep. Tape and play monotonous sounds such as the vacuum cleaner, washing machine, a ticking clock or running water, or try some peaceful birdsong or harmonious classical music.

hunger cry

Probably the easiest to recognize, the hunger cry is longer than other cries and can cause your baby to gulp in air, which is not good before a feed, especially for a colicky baby. Rising in intensity, this cry is usually accompanied by fist sucking and rooting against your chest. Even if your

baby only fed an hour ago, it is possible that the is hungry again. If you can spot the physical body language, sometimes it will be possible to anticipate and avoid the crying stage.

angry cry

Long, loud, piercing and nerve-wracking, this cry is sometimes accompanied by a trembling body. Your baby may be frightened and in need of some cuddles, even though they are rejected at the same time. Take a deep breath and feel strong and positive. Use your voice calmly 'ssshhing', talking, singing or humming, which helps to keep you calm too. You could stroke or pick her up, jiggle her or try to divert her attention visually with exaggerated facial expressions. Walking around with her in your arms or over your shoulder may calm her down.

pain

Shrill, shrieking and long, this cry may be accompanied by a tense rigid body, flailing fists, eyes squeezed tight shut, and in the case of colic, knees drawn up. Pick your baby up and look for the source of the pain. If she is hot, wipe over her with a cool, not cold, flannel. If you cannot find the source of the pain and the crying continues, call your doctor.

Above *Learning to distinguish your baby's different cries will help you cope with her demands.*

FEBRILE FIT

Febrile fits are often due to internal overheating because of an infection. If her eyes are rolling and she appears to shiver or tremble, your baby may not necessarily be cold. This could be the beginning of a febrile fit. In this instance your baby needs instant medical attention, and any resulting convulsions should not be restrained. Put your baby in a safe place (on a blanket on the floor) and try to keep her cool while waiting for the doctor.

handling your baby

Babies are at times quite soft. At other times they manage to rigidly defy all efforts to place them into their car seat or cot. There are a number of techniques that you can use to make handling your baby safe, comfortable and comforting, always remembering to firmly support a young baby's neck and head.

Above *Talking to your baby both during and before you handle him (even if he does not appear to understand you), can help prepare him for movement of some kind.*

LOTS OF ATTENTION

Remember, a baby that is only picked up when crying, learns that this is the way to get your attention. Give your baby lots of attention always, not just when he needs or demands it.

lifting and lowering

To lift and lower your newborn, first think of your back and bend your knees. Then slide one arm under your baby's neck and head and the other under his back and bottom, sliding him towards you. When lying him down again make sure you support his head in the same way, placing his lower body first and easing his neck, shoulders and head last, sliding your hands out gently and tenderly.

Your baby's movements may be quite jerky, uncontrolled and sudden, and surprisingly stiff, so you do need a reasonably firm hold on him.

Always try to keep your movements slow and gentle, and look at your baby the whole time so you can keep eye contact and talk to him.

getting close

There are plenty of ways to get close to your baby. Babies usually like to be close to your chest, where they can hear the familiar sound of your heartbeat. Again use two hands, one supporting the lower body and the other cradling the head and neck. Draw your baby to you and rest his head on your shoulder.

Alternatively, when sitting you can let your baby lie sideways against your body, supported by an encircling arm, with his head on your chest. He may like to lie on his tummy over your knees. You can try sitting propped up by cushions, with your knees raised, resting your baby's back against your legs and his feet on your tummy, looking right at you. Have soft cushions or pillows either side of your legs, in case he decides to throw himself sideways. Lying down you can cuddle up together. Most babies like skin-to-skin cuddles, they usually have a strong sense of smell and are very familiar with your odour.

Colicky babies may well like to be held higher up your body, almost up over your shoulder, which possibly relieves some of the discomfort in their tummy.

the uncuddly baby

Babies that don't like to be cuddled stiffen and arch backwards, and are difficult to hold. Carry him with his back and head against your tummy, so he faces forwards. Place your arms under his knees to help relax him. Try laying him over your legs or lap, face down, and gently stroking or patting his back.

reassuring your baby

Some babies are particularly scared of moving, since while in the womb their movements were restricted by the size of the mother's uterus. Simply being lifted out of a cot or from the floor to your chest must feel like freefalling in space to a newborn, so take time to reassure him as you pick him up. At first he may dislike being held at arms' length, so keep him close. Soon you will be able to enjoy more exciting and stimulating play movements with him, like holding him up high, a game he will enjoy as much, if not more, than you, and he will reward you with gleeful chuckles and sounds that you love to hear.

Above Fully support your baby's head and neck as this area may be retaining tension from the birth.

TAKING CARE OF YOU

While carrying a baby standing up, try not to arch your back too much. You will find yourself having to alter your point of balance with the extra weight. The other danger to avoid is carrying your baby on one hip all the time.

Try to alternate hips, as at the moment you probably have one preferred side.

rocking and motion

There are three reasons to rock or swing your baby: to lull her to sleep; to amuse her; and to help ease wind through her body. There are also a number of ways to rock or soothe your baby with motion, including carrying her in a sling, putting her in a baby bouncer, rocking her in a chair or cradle, or even driving her around in the car.

Above *If your baby is soothed by being held close to you, feeling your movement, the best thing to do is attach her to you, as many native peoples do.*

carrying your baby

There are different designs of slings that you can use to keep your baby with you while you move around. Some position the baby looking at you, others allow your baby to look out at what is going on. Slings also keep babies upright, which can help wind to pass through the body.

These slings leave your hands free, so if your back is strong, you can get on with all sorts of activities while carrying your baby with you. The combination of the monotonous sound of the vacuum cleaner, for example, and your movements will soothe her off to sleep in no time.

bouncers

Babies need to be laid flat, or close to it, for the first three months, but they can spend some time in reclining bouncing chairs, set to the lowest recline position. The chair lets her make the movements herself, although it will take a while for her to realize this. As your baby's muscles develop you can adjust the position of the chair so that she begins to sit up and can see more of what is going on around her. When choosing a bouncer, make sure visual attachments are removable, to avoid overstimulation when it is time to rest.

rockers

The movement of a rocker is often slower, less jerky and smoother than a bouncer. Most babies like the gentle swinging and it rocks them off to sleep. Of course you can replicate the same sensation and gentle, lulling movement by holding your baby in your arms while you rock in a rocking chair, or buy a rocking cradle for your baby to sleep in.

bouncing harnesses

Harnesses usually hang in a doorway and can usually be used from the age of three to four months, once your baby can support her head firmly. They support your baby's back and neck and can be gently swung to and fro.

ROCKING COLICKY BABIES

Colicky babies are always on the move, trying to get rid of the pain that they are feeling. Movement allows wind to dissipate, but your baby also needs to be high up on your shoulder, so that her cramping tummy presses against your bonier part. Alternatively, she may like to lie with her tummy on your forearm and chest on your open palm, and be rocked from side to side.

the car

Most babies are easily soothed to sleep in the car. The sound of the engine and the feeling of the car moving are very relaxing. Some babies might need to have the added visual stimulation removed, so drape a blanket over the window if necessary.

Going for a drive with your baby can prove to be the perfect way to calm an inconsolably crying baby, but only do this at night if you feel alert enough to do so. You do not want to risk having an accident because you are too tired.

If your baby does fall asleep in the car, you cannot guarantee that she won't wake up again as soon as you arrive back home, but for the peace and quiet it is still worth a try.

OVERSTIMULATION

Babies can be overstimulated by bouncing and will soon get fed up and start to cry. Only rock or gently bounce your baby if it is soothing and comforting her.

bathing

Babies don't need to be bathed every day since they don't get very dirty. The main reason to bring bathing into your daily routine is for fun and pleasure. Your baby has been used to being in warm water in the womb, so for most babies a bath is a soothing and calming experience.

Above *Bathtime can be very relaxing, even for small babies. Make sure that you have plenty of warm towels and avoid drafty rooms.*

Babies can be bathed in their own baby bath, or join you or your partner in the main bath. Most babies do not like being undressed, so be prepared for a few tears. They will get used to this sensation, so rest assured that undressing will not always be a distressing experience.

If, on the other hand, your baby is actually frightened of the water, you may choose topping and tailing (see page 42) instead.

preparation for after the bath

Your baby still has no way to regulate her temperature, so it is important that she is not allowed to cool down after a bath. Make sure the room is warm and has no draughts. Have a few soft towels to hand, not just one, and if possible let them warm over a radiator. You also need to have a clean nappy and clothes ready, so you can gently – but reasonably quickly – dress your baby again.

It can be a good idea to lay a large soft towel over your lap and up your front, both to protect your clothes from splashes and so that your baby has a soft surface to cuddle up to when you take her out of the bath.

using a baby bath

If your baby bath does not have a stand, place it on a non-slip surface, at about hip height, so that it is comfortable for your back. Only fill the bath up to 10 cm (4 in). Always test the water with your elbow or a thermometer; it should be warm not hot, and no hotter than 29°C (84°F).

Undress your baby, leaving her nappy on, and swaddle her in a soft, warm towel. Gently wipe over her face with a warm flannel.

Next attend to the nappy and clean her bottom with cotton wool and warm water, keeping the towel wrapped around your baby's top half. Unwrap the towel and support your naked baby with your dominant hand under her hips, your other hand under her shoulders, with her head in the crook of your arm and your fingers under her armpit.

Right Start to put your baby in the bath feet first, then lower her slowly into the water, supporting her head and back.

Talk or sing to her and retain eye contact to reassure her and alert yourself to any impending cries. Give lots of smiles of encouragement as you gently place her feet and legs into the water. Slide your hand from under her hips, still supporting her with your other arm.

Use your free hand to splash water over her body. Your baby does not need to be in the bath for very long at all, and if she gets particularly distressed during bathing simply take her out. Wrap her in a warm towel and gently pat her dry before dressing.

If she enjoys the familiar feeling of warm water on her skin she may want to kick, so let her play and enjoy the bathing experience.

bathing together

Taking a bath with a parent is enjoyable for your baby, and can involve the kind of loving touches that are important to a baby's development. This is also a good choice if your baby does not like the water as she is likely to be reassured by the contact with your skin. It is a good idea to have another person present when bathing together, so that they can safely pass your baby to you and take her before you get out.

Place a non-slip mat in the bath and fill with enough warm water to just cover you both. Test the water with your elbow or a thermometer to ensure it is no hotter than 29°C (84°F). It is not advisable to use essential oils during these bathtimes since they can make the bath a little slippery.

When bathing together, aim to keep your baby close to you, creating a sense of security, as babies usually love the feeling of your skin next to theirs. You could hold your baby to your chest and belly while gently stroking her back and singing or humming to her.

When she is more confident you can bend your knees and lay her against your thighs with her legs on your tummy, looking at you. Do not stay in the bath for too long: if your baby gets upset or the water temperature begins to drop, it is time to get out.

CRYING DURING THE BATH

If your baby cries during the bath, he probably feels a little unsure, so offer all sorts of murmured, smiling coos. Run your fingers in the water so that he hears the sound and sees the drops. Try to keep his attention diverted by scooping water up and letting it fall over his feet and legs.

If he cannot be diverted and is obviously unhappy, lift him out, wrap him in a towel and cuddle him to reassure him. Try again in a few days, or try topping and tailing for a few weeks.

hair washing

If your baby does not like having his hair washed, it is a good idea to wash it separately from the rest of his body, so he doesn't associate the unpleasantness of hair washing with the fun of bathtime.

Position the baby bath in a safe place and pour a little warm water in. You do not need to use a shampoo, but if you want to you can add a little rose water. Remove your baby's top and wrap him in a towel. Hold your baby to your side, supporting his head, neck and shoulders with one arm, leaving your dominant hand for the washing. Gently lean over the baby bath and drizzle the warm water over his forehead and scalp.

Keep your baby warm in the towel and gently pat his head dry. Regular soft brushing also cleans the hair.

topping and tailing

For the baby that is especially scared or really dislikes water, a general sponge down is a good alternative to bathtime. Your baby's skin has the ability to self-clean, so a wipe all over is sufficient.

The advantage of this type of wash is that your baby remains partially clothed at all times, which is helpful if he does not like the feel of air against

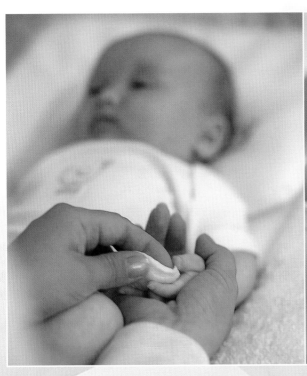

his skin. Your baby may like to sit on a towel on your lap, or prefer to lie on a mat or a sheepskin rug, which is soft and warm. While topping and tailing you can sing, hum or chat to your baby to reassure and distract him.

Above *Topping and tailing is an option for a baby who doesn't like a bath. Start at the head and work your way down.*

the top half

Fill a bowl with warm water and have a sponge ready. Remove the clothes from your baby's top half only, talking all the time. You do not need a very wet sponge. Gently wipe over your baby's chest, neck and arms.

Pat your baby dry before leaning him forwards onto your forearm, if on your lap, or turning him over on the mat. Wipe over his back. Pat his back dry and put the clothes on again before you start the lower half.

the lower half

With the top half warm and dressed, take off his socks and wipe over his feet, working in between the toes where fluff can get stuck. Put clean socks on and remove the rest of his clothes. If your baby is on your lap you can guarantee that he will pee, but it doesn't matter since he is on a towel anyway.

Wipe over his legs and pat dry. Re-dress your clean baby, giving him lots of kisses and cuddles for being so good.

nappies

You will find that you change your young baby up to ten times a day, so make sure that you talk or sing to her to make this a more enjoyable time. Also be prepared – have everything that you need within reach so that you can change your baby quickly as often she will not like having her skin exposed to the air.

disposable or reusable nappies?

There are two main types of nappy: disposable and reusable. Reusable fabric nappies take time to rinse, wash and sterilize, but can work out cheaper than disposable ones. They are also more ecologically friendly than disposable nappies which don't biodegrade, although you will be using detergent and electricity to wash (and dry) the fabric nappies.

Disposable nappies are convenient and are easier to use than fabric nappies as they don't need to be sterilized or washed. However, they work out to be more expensive than reusable nappies, and most aren't biodegradable and therefore aren't ecologically friendly.

when should I change my baby?

There is no ideal time to change your baby's nappy, but as a rule you should change nappies often (around every two hours during the day and a little less often at night). Some babies have particularly delicate skin and need their nappies changed as soon as they are wet. Others can get away with being changed after a feed.

Below *Many babies do not like having their skin exposed to the air for any length of time. Have everything ready and change her quickly.*

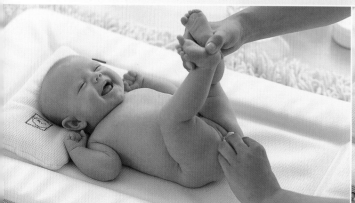
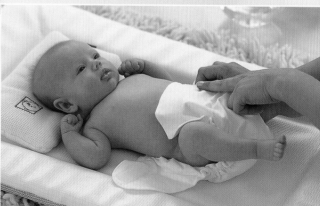

be prepared

As with bathing, you need to have everything to hand before you start to undress your baby and change the nappy. This means being close to a nappy bin and having some cotton wool and a bowl of warm water, a soft towel or changing mat and the nappies close by. You can change your baby on a mat or on a towel on the floor. If you are using a changing table keep one hand on your baby at all times. Once confident, you will be able to change the nappy with your baby on your lap.

changing the nappy

Always wash your hands before and after changing a nappy. Undo the nappy and use the front of it to clean up most of the mess if your baby is dirty. Roll up the nappy and place to one side. Then, gently holding your baby's legs up, use the cotton wool and warm water to clean the area completely and carefully. With girls, clean from front to back to keep germs away from the vagina. Clean boys around the penis and testicles. Pat your baby's skin dry with cotton wool or a towel before putting on a clean nappy.

checking the contents of the nappy

It is a good idea to check your baby's nappy – if the stools are unusually dry then check that she is getting enough liquid. The number of stools your baby passes and what they look like will depend on whether your baby is bottle fed or breastfed.

nappy rash

Nappy rash is a common complaint that is caused when a baby's skin is affected by the urine in a wet nappy reacting with bacteria in the faeces. To try and prevent nappy rash make sure that you change your baby's nappy regularly, and let the air get to your baby's bottom as often as possible – after her bath or after removing a dirty nappy and cleaning her bottom, leave her to play without a nappy on.

disposing of nappies and waste

Whether you are using reusable or disposable nappies, always put the contents down the toilet. With reusable nappies the liners can be flushed away, but never put disposable nappies down the toilet. Reusable nappies should be placed in a nappy bucket for soaking, while disposable nappies should be placed in a nappy sack and disposed of in the rubbish bin.

Above Use cotton wool and warm water to clean the nappy area. Pat dry before putting on a clean nappy.

CONNECTING

Remember to talk, sing or hum to your baby when you change her nappy, making this a loving time, rather than simply a duty. Nappy changing can provide a good opportunity to massage your baby. Once she is cleaned up and before putting on a clean nappy, massage her feet, legs or tummy, or all three, following the instructions on pages 77–79 and 86–93.

dressing

Dressing babies is about keeping them comfortable and either warm or cool depending on their environment. It is also about choosing the kind of clothes that make a parent's life easier, for example, ones that are easily washable and simple to take off and put on, as children often dislike being dressed.

Above *Choose garments of natural fibres that are easy to take off and that allow your baby's skin to breathe.*

what to wear

Keeping warm or cool and comfortable is of the utmost importance, so choose soft garments, made from natural fibres – such as cotton – that allow air to circulate, letting your baby's skin breathe, and provide freedom of movement. Synthetic fibres make the body hot and may cause your baby to be uncomfortable or even overheat. For practical reasons make sure all clothes are machine-washable and that they are easy to put on: front fastening is the best option for ease of use. Sleepsuits are the obvious choice for newborns because they are easy to put on, comfortable, unlikely to irritate the skin and do not need to be completely removed for nappy changing.

Layering clothes is the best option for regulating temperature. A cardigan over a sleepsuit can easily be removed if she gets too warm. When going from indoors to outdoors it is a good idea to take light cotton or wool blankets that can be added and taken away as necessary.

A lot of body heat is lost through the head, so hats are a necessity in cold weather. Babies should also wear sun hats to protect them from the intensity of the sun's rays, while light cotton wraps will help keep your baby's temperature less erratic in the hot weather. Remember, however, that babies should not be exposed to direct sunlight.

crying while dressing

Babies often cry when having their clothes taken off or put on. This may simply be because they do not like the interruption that fiddling around with clothes entails. Also, nearly all newborns dislike the feeling of air on their skin. Don't worry though, they will get used to this sensation and even begin to enjoy the freedom of being naked. However, do pay attention to your baby's cries or whimpers, in case they indicate discomfort in a particular area of the body that you will want to check with a doctor.

If crying babies are not soft, they are stiff and rigid, there is no in-between. Keep up the happy smiling face and the baby chatter and try

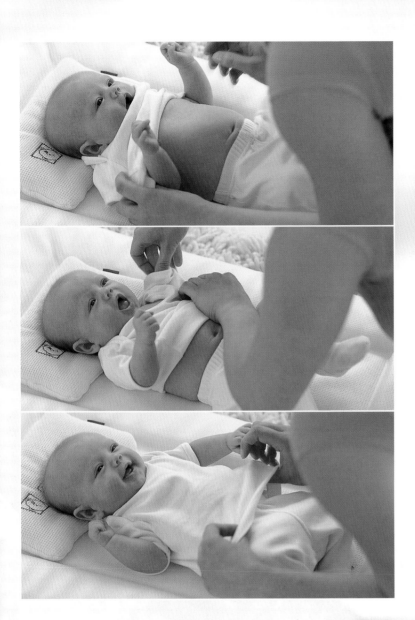

Left When dressing and undressing, maintain eye contact with your baby and continue to talk to her throughout the process.

DOS AND DON'TS OF DRESSING

- Don't try to dress your baby immediately after a feed.
- Do pick your baby up and give her a cuddle if she is starting to become anxious.
- Don't be in a hurry.
- Do let your baby have a kick around while undressed and unrestricted.
- Don't buy lacy fabrics that her fingers can get caught in.
- Do check for loose buttons.

WHERE TO DRESS

Always dress your baby in a warm room and away from draughts. Make sure you have the nappy and clothes ready, and if you are dressing her on a changing table make sure you keep a hand on her at all times. Natural sheepskin makes a good mat to lay your baby on since it is very soft and warming: your baby has no means of temperature control so gets cold quickly with no clothes on. Sheepskin is also cooling in the summer and easy to wash.

giving her a tickle, or burying your head into her tummy and blowing a raspberry on it. Touch your baby lovingly as you begin to dress or undress her, and keep up the eye contact. These measures will distract your baby from the actions of dressing and let her feel secure. You can pick your baby up and give her a cuddle, or try dressing her sitting on your lap: in time and with practice you will do this easily.

Remember that it is perfectly normal for a baby to cry while dressing. So try not to get flustered and know that dressing will not always be a problem.

sleep

You may be amazed at the amount of time that your newborn baby spends asleep, although it is not always at the times that you would like. Parents need to adapt to the routine of their newborn, until the baby begins to appreciate the difference between night and day.

Above *Sometimes your baby may not be able to sleep because she is too hot or too cold – make adjustments to her coverings to compensate.*

routines

Your baby will not necessarily need the same amount of sleep every day. If there is a lot going on he may well feel the excitement and be more awake. Your baby is adaptable. Although routines are important and you want him to understand the difference between night and day, he can stand the occasional alteration, and you will be happier and more relaxed if you are not always clock-watching.

Make sure any routine suits you and your family. For example, if your partner comes home from work close to your baby's bedtime, this will excite him, which is not a conducive state for settling down. So allocate time in the routine for playing, followed by a calm-down time.

why isn't my baby sleeping?

There are any number of reasons why a baby might not be a good sleeper, by day or night. Newborns are unable to regulate their body temperature for the first few months, so she may simply be too hot or cold. Check his temperature with the back of your hand on his neck or with a thermometer and add or remove blankets as necessary.

Sometimes, partly due to the fact that he cannot control his temperature, his skin may be dry and itchy. Preterm babies have much more sensitive skin, while overdue babies may have more wrinkled and dried skin. In both cases massaging with all natural pure oils would moisturize, nourish and soothe the skin.

Spicy foods, if breastfeeding, might have been delicious to you, but be playing havoc with your baby's under-functioning digestive system. It takes up to three months to develop the muscles used to digest, which may account for the mysterious disappearance of colic after that time.

Sometimes your baby just does not feel safe. A reassuring, loving hug from you is most needed, along with soft words and a little rocking. Swaddling can bring your baby a sense of security.

helping your baby to sleep

Perhaps your baby can hear interesting noises outside or is stimulated by a colourful mobile above the cot. Remove any distractions and play some background noise. This will also drown out any other intrusive noises. Television is stimulating and should not be used to put a baby to sleep.

Unfortunately, he may simply be hungry . . . again. Even if you have only recently fed him, it does absolutely no harm to try again. Remember, however, that caffeine is passed on through your milk and exacerbates insomnia. It is present in cola drinks, tea, coffee, chocolate, many over-the-counter drugs and any product where it is used as a flavouring.

If you are breastfeeding you can let your baby sleep in bed with you. Once you have fed and cuddled him, you can put him back in his cot. You will find that even while you are asleep you can anticipate his needs, and all it needs is a whimper from him to wake you. Don't worry, this habit can be broken later, as the feeds become less frequent. It is highly unlikely that you will roll over onto your baby, as many people fear, but you must put up a bed guard rail to stop your baby falling out and you should not bring your baby into your bed if either you or your partner have been either drinking alcohol, smoking, taking drugs or are very tired.

Above When your baby needs to feed every hour (and some do), do consider letting him sleep with you.

A MOTHER'S SLEEP

You need your sleep just like your baby does, so whenever he takes a nap, you need to do the same. Don't use your baby's sleeping time to catch up with the chores. The housework can wait, and can even be done with a baby who is awake and in a sling. The more relaxed you can be, the more content your baby will feel.

the nursery

The nursery should feel like a comfortable haven, with a peaceful atmosphere, to calm you as well as your baby. If you are painting the nursery for your new arrival then think about the colours that you like and find soothing, and that will help to create a tranquil bedroom in which your child will happily sleep.

Above *Soft, peaceful colours in the nursery will help promote relaxation and sleep. An uncluttered room will mean that your baby is not kept awake by distracting visual stimulation.*

creating the right environment

If your baby is in the nursery, make this a comfortable space with a peaceful, uncluttered atmosphere. Her room needs to be kept clean and warm, but not stiflingly hot; it should be aired daily by opening the windows when she is not in there. Position the cot away from draughts and keep the lighting subdued.

choosing colour

Most parents choose soft, cool pastel shades to decorate the walls of their baby's bedroom. There is a reason for this: bright vibrant colours are stimulating and more suitable for a room where your baby will be awake, such as the play area. (For more on the ways in which colours can affect mood, see panel opposite.)

natural furnishings

The more natural the atmosphere in your baby's room, the easier it will be for her to feel relaxed there. Avoid artificial materials that may give off subtle fumes or build up a charge of static electricity which could compromise your child's health. Check what type of materials are used in the soft furnishings including bedding, curtains, carpet, rugs and cushions, and consider replacing synthetic fibres with cotton or linen.

peace and quiet

Sudden noises can startle babies, while regular noises become familiar and help them to feel secure – after all, it was quite noisy inside your womb! Particular sounds, such as repeatedly humming a single soft tone can reassure your baby. There are also many cassettes and CDs that promote sleep and relaxation. These are usually recorded to a particular beat that relates to our dreaming state, and are designed to be played quietly in the background.

Far left Soothing, calming, antiseptic lavender ushers in a relaxing atmosphere.

Left Suncatchers placed in the window of the nursery create beautiful rainbows on the walls, ceiling and floor.

aromatherapy

The two oils most often advised for babies are lavender and roman chamomile. Add one drop of oil to a small bowl of water placed on a radiator or in a bowl of steaming water on the floor. The aroma will relax your baby and she will begin to associate these fragrances with sleep time. Never place the water close to your baby's head or within her reach.

using crystals

A beautiful natural crystal, as well as being decorative, can help to balance energies. Rose quartz, symbolizing love, is especially recommended for babies and children and is said to alleviate fear. Pink is also associated with the heart and friendship so could help to create a joyous, soft space.

Consider placing a 'suncatcher' in your baby's nursery window. These beautiful pieces of multi-faceted glass crystal are designed to catch the light and project coloured beams onto the walls and ceiling of the room. If you hang them from a hook you can gently spin them so that different hues sweep around the room. This creates a magical effect that will enhance your baby's feeling of well-being and keep them captivated.

Some parents place a salt crystal lamp as a comforting night light in their children's room. It emits a reassuring pinkish-orange glow and the negative ions emitted by the lamp help to neutralize harmful positive ions generated by electrical equipment in the home.

COLOUR THERAPY

Colour therapists attribute different properties to colours:

● BLUE is associated with serenity, peace and truth, and calms the electromagnetic fields around the body.

● GREEN is harmonious and soothing, and considered to be the primary colour for the nervous system, toning and calming the mind, body and spirit.

● PINK calms the spirit and has a positive effect when used to heal difficult relationships or communication problems. Using a pink lightbulb in a bedside lamp is recommended to combat insomnia in adults.

● LILAC aids relaxation. It is considered to be the colour of creativity that enhances the natural intuitive instincts.

feeding

A baby can have all his nutritional needs met by milk alone for the first six months. Breast-milk is best, but not all new mothers find it easy or possible to breastfeed – remember that if you are having problems breastfeeding then you can express your milk and feed your baby your breast-milk from a bottle.

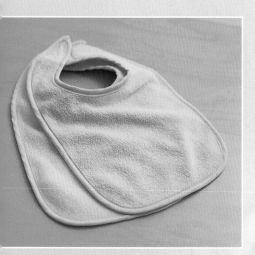

Above *Babies' clothes can be protected easily with natural cotton bibs, as all babies tend to bring a little milk back up after their feed.*

breastfeeding

Human milk is perfectly designed for our young. It contains all the nutrients a baby needs, is rich in antibodies to protect against infections and contains high levels of the essential fat DHA – which promotes brain development – minerals for healthy bones, protein for growth and fat-soluble vitamins that are easily absorbed. Babies absorb breast-milk better than formula milk, and through it get more nourishing nutritional value into their bodies.

latching on

Some babies simply open their mouths, find the nipple and suckle. For other mothers breastfeeding is more difficult and can take practice and perseverance. Give yourself time to relax and trust your instincts. When breastfeeding is relaxed it is also a great aid to bonding.

Breastfeeding is often easier if you put your baby to the breast within a few minutes of giving birth. Your baby may need a little help to start suckling, especially if he was premature. Encourage him to take in the nipple and as much of the areola (or brown skin) as possible. You could try expressing a little milk as you guide him to your nipple so that he can smell it.

About three to five days after giving birth, the initial colostrum – which provides your baby with all the nutrients and antibodies to prevent infection – is replaced by milk. Your production of milk is stimulated by your baby's sucking, so frequent feeding ensures that your milk supply continues. You should let your baby suck on the first side for as long as he wants, to ensure that he receives both foremilk – the dilute, thirst-quenching milk – and hindmilk – the richer, creamier milk.

bottle feeding

For some women breastfeeding is simply not an option. For the bottle-fed baby there is a wide range of milk formulas to choose from, including

Above *Whether breast- or bottle feeding, always make sure that you are in a comfortable position which allows you and your baby to feel connected.*

organic milks that are the best choice. If your baby is premature, consult your doctor for alternatives which may be more suitable for an immature digestive system.

Always read the ingredients contained in bought milk. It is not necessary for your baby to have sugar or glucose in his formula. The milk should contain manganese, chromium and selineum and high levels of zinc, essential vitamins and minerals.

When bottle feeding it can be a good idea to give your baby water. Sometimes he may be just thirsty, not hungry.

burping

Babies cough and splutter, posset (bring back up a little milk) and have a certain amount of wind after feeding. Burping is a way of bringing up any air your baby has swallowed while feeding or crying, which may cause discomfort later. Not all babies benefit from being burped, so don't feel that you have to burp your baby after every feed if it doesn't seem to help.

If you think your baby has taken in a lot of air, the best position to burp him in is against your shoulder. Put a cloth over your shoulder to protect your clothes and gently rub his back. Alternatively you can try sitting him on your lap, leaning him forward slightly. A rubbing motion is preferable to firm patting. Some babies do not take in as much wind as others, so it is not necessary to sit for ages waiting for a burp to surface.

MAKING THE MOST OF YOUR BREAST-MILK

A mother's milk is only as good as her diet and the amount of rest that she is getting. Here are some tips to ensure you are giving your baby the best milk you can.

● Avoid strenuous exercise before a feed, it may alter the taste of your milk.

● Regain your energy with three proper meals a day – you will not put on weight, but your baby will. Choose organic produce whenever possible.

● Drink water. Your baby will take about 1.2 litres (2 pints) from you daily, so you should drink about 3 litres (5¼ pints) a day.

● If your baby does not seem satisfied with your milk, eat a little more protein. This does not have to be in the form of meat or cheese. Try soya, wholegrains, pulses, beans, rice, seeds or fish.

● Do not have caffeine or spicy foods before your baby's night feed. Passed through to your breast-milk these can stimulate babies so they don't sleep.

smell and taste

The senses of smell and taste are closely related to each other, and to memory. This memory-gathering experience begins in the womb, since at 24 weeks your baby will begin to absorb odours and flavours transmitted through the amniotic fluid. Once born, your unique body scent will be comforting to your baby.

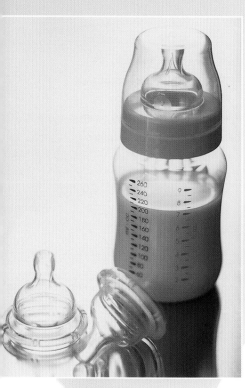

Above *When possible, express your own breast-milk for bottle feeding.*

smell and memory

From the moment of birth your baby receives information on her surroundings through her sense of smell, and she is highly sensitive to a small range of smells. Within one hour she will recognize and locate your nipple, due to the smell of your milk. This smell stays in her memory and allows her to thrive. At two weeks of age she can distinguish between your milk and that of another mother.

comforting scents

Your distinctive body aroma sends messages of comfort and protection to your baby, while her scent stimulates your milk production and is a strong motivator for attachment. For most babies, especially bottle-fed babies who do not experience the scent at the nipple, the body scent around the neck is an important identifier. With this in mind you may choose to avoid wearing strong perfumes or aftershave, which can lead to confusion and desensitization. Your baby can become quite attached to the many aromas on a familiar security item, and prefer that it remains unwashed. She may like to have such items placed close to her when she feels unsettled.

taste and memory

The sense of taste is highly developed at birth, and your baby will prefer a sweet taste. Your breast-milk tastes sweet, so she will want to suckle. Disliking sour or bitter flavours is a way of distinguishing poisonous substances.

first foods

Your baby's nutritional needs are adequately met by milk for the first six months. At about this time you may notice that she is still hungry after a milk feed, that she demands more milk or that she starts to wake up in the night for extra feeds. These signals indicate when you should start to introduce weaning foods.

Above Babies seem to like the smell of vanilla and banana. Both are quite sweet, as is breast milk.

PREPARING PURÉES

The best way to ensure that your baby's food does not contain added salt or sugar is to prepare it yourself. Steam or boil organic washed vegetables with their skin on to get maximum goodness, then peel and thoroughly purée. Babies who have just started weaning do not like lumps.

Puréed vegetables and fruit (preferably organic) make excellent first weaning foods. These new flavours should be introduced individually. At this time your main goal is not trying to fill her up, but developing her taste buds, so try offering her a teaspoon of purée, say carrot or banana, in between milk feeds. Give her the same food for several consecutive days, in order to observe any allergic reactions. You can add a familiar smell to the food, to encourage tasting, by adding just a little breast-milk to the mix. Always introduce new foods and tastes on their own, before putting different flavours together.

Although your baby likes the sweet flavour of milk, do not add sugar or honey to any of her foods. It is not necessary and will encourage her to have a sweet tooth. The same is true of salt, which you should never add to the food you prepare for your baby. In fact, when it comes to solid foods, your baby will prefer bland flavours, and you don't want to bombard her newly developing sense of taste.

CHOKING

If your baby starts to choke, look inside her mouth and, if you can see it, try to hook out the obstruction with your finger, while gently slapping her back. If the object is not easy to reach or not visible, lay her over your arm with her head supported in your hand and pointing downwards, and gently slap her back until the obstruction is dislodged.

sight

Babies can see about 20–25 cm (8–10 in) when they are born, although they will not be able to focus clearly. The colour of your baby's eyes will gradually change and so will his ability to distinguish colours. He can see in colour from birth, but will focus better with just black and white or strong contrasting colours at first.

DEVELOPING VISUAL AWARENESS

You can help to activate your baby's eyesight development by placing a mobile above his cot. Position black and white pictures, or pictures using strong, contrasting colours where he can see them, but not close enough to grab. If you believe you have a visually stimulated baby, however, leave the cot free of diversions to help encourage sleep.

treasuring

Newborn babies' sight is not totally focussed, but they can see you and lock into your eyes while you are cradling them. One of the loveliest things that you and your baby can do is spend time in the depths of eye exploration, when deep primal feelings of softness, love and protection will flow through your body. It is a wonderful experience for you both to alternate between looking and holding, treasuring your baby close to your skin.

boys and girls

Newborn girls are seemingly far more responsive to visual stimili than newborn boys. A girl will be fascinated by your facial expressions and more easily pacified by seeing your face. Boys on the other hand become more visually stimulated over a period of time. So you may be able to stop your little girl crying completely using exaggerated facial expressions, but for the boy this will cause a temporary lull only, before you have to find something else to distract him with.

playing games

By his second month your new baby will be using his sight a lot more. He will start to follow you around with his eyes, but will still be most fascinated with your face and expressions. He will be intrigued by mobiles and by toys that you dangle near his face or hands. He will start to gain more control over his arms and may want to touch objects that he is drawn to.

From two months onwards he will start to get great enjoyment, fun and laughter out of simple games involving you hiding your eyes behind your hands. Blowing raspberries or sticking your tongue out is also a form of interactive enjoyment. These games are not only fun for you both, they develop your baby's awareness and his eye muscles. As his eye muscle control develops so does his curiosity, balance, coordination and language.

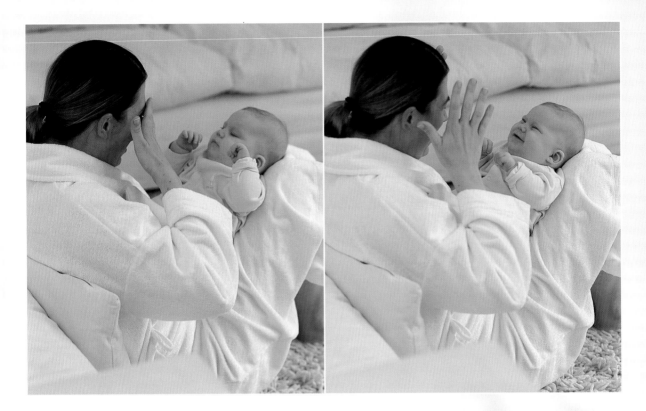

the visually stimulated baby

One sense can be more dominant than others. A very alert baby that is always looking around, gets upset when he can't see you or an object, or stays absolutely still, staring at one object for ages, is probably visually stimulated. He will learn best by actively seeing how something is done. As a baby he will want to look at pictures and inspect and hold things for some length of time. He might need to have a sheet draped around his cot, pram or car seat on a car journey to block out light and shadows, since too many things to look at could make him very agitated, especially when he is tired and can't switch off.

training the eye muscles

As your baby gets older and is able to follow the movements of your hand, if there are any problems, such as a squint or one eye not moving with the other, then you could try the slow-working non-invasive eye exercises specific to The Bates Method. These are based on restoring the natural ability of the eyes. Eyesight can also be improved with co-ordinated body movements, such as those found within the Brain Gym (www.braingym.org).

Above Playing visual games with your baby helps to develop a bond between you and also trains your baby's eye muscles.

hearing

The first sense to fully develop in a baby is hearing, so the sound and feeling of your voice soon have the power to relax and uplift your child. Chatter away to her while you do the chores, point out what you are doing and sing songs and repeat nursery rhymes to her to stimulate her to copy you verbally.

Above *This singing Tibetan bowl produces a complete range of notes simultaneously. It is a good way to communicate with a deaf baby, who will feel the notes reverberating.*

Your baby has been listening to your muffled sounds and language from inside your womb. Although she did not understand the meaning of the sounds, she could feel your reactions to them, whether loud and harsh, happy, relaxed, loving or everyday. She has built up a subconscious awareness that these sounds cause chemical changes inside that feel either good or bad. You can therefore calm and connect with your baby by using the kind of sounds that feel good to her.

pitch

Babies seem to prefer higher and softer pitches. They also soon learn when you are upset from any slight deviation in your voice, so if you are feeling tired or stressed it is often best just to be silent and just hold your baby lovingly instead of talking to her.

repetition

You can help the development of the temporal lobe, relevant to hearing and speech, by repeating all manner of sounds. Constant repetition helps babies to understand that words actually mean something and relate to objects or people.

gender differences

Hearing is different in boys and girls. Generally, newborn boys have less acute hearing than girls and they do not seem to be able to locate the source of a sound as well as girls do. This means that any comforting, soothing sounds that you make for your son will need to be done for longer and you will need to be closer to him, before you get the desired response.

the sound-stimulated baby

We all develop one sense a little more than the others, and this will affect how easily we learn later in life. The baby who likes sound will grow into

Right Pointing to objects as you read to your child helps her develop a sense of language.

the child who learns best by hearing someone explaining, not by seeing it done or by trying to do it. As a baby, however, she can get very distressed by being overloaded. She will like certain sounds, but may get unreasonable if that sound continues beyond her time endurance, which could be as short as 40 seconds, and what she liked yesterday, she doesn't like today. A sound-stimulated baby may well be vocal herself, with a very loud scream. She may be difficult to settle since she is unable to tune out noise, in which case some soft, droning noise in the background (see page 60) that blocks out other, more stimulating sounds could help her to settle and relax.

talking to your baby

In order to learn our spoken language, your baby needs to hear it constantly (although not from the television!). Talking to your baby as you go about your everyday tasks will encourage her to speak from an early age, and as her vision develops you can point at things when you name them, or tell your baby what you are doing. Your baby will try to copy what you are saying in her own time, and she may also try to sing along to a song. Do not mistake these attempts at communication as a cry and try to stifle them. Allow her to chatter away in her own baby babble, encourage her attempts to speak, and she will soon pick up your language (see also page 60). Sight, speech and hearing are extremely closely linked and work together to teach your baby about her world and how she can communicate this.

There is also a way of commmunicating with your baby without words known as Makaton, which is a unique and international form of sign language that incorporates the symbolic description of the whole action and not just of the actual verb. This is widely recognized as being the quickest and easiest form of sign language to learn from an early age for both parent and baby.

HEARING IMPAIRMENTS

A baby that is slow to respond to your voice, especially when you are not in her line of vision, or is startled when you appear in front of her, may have a hearing impairment. If you are concerned about your baby's hearing, you need to consult your doctor.

If your child is deaf it is essential that you learn to sign, so that everyone can communicate and your baby feels understood. A deaf baby can feel sound vibrations, so you can still sing or hum while cuddling her.

sounds to lull or stimulate

What babies hear can affect their moods, so soft sounds and calming background noises can be employed to help soothe a tense child or tired baby that simply can't switch off. Correspondingly, exaggerating your tone while speaking to your baby will stimulate and interest her and keep her attention for longer.

Above *Soothing background sounds – such as wind chimes – can be easily incorporated into your home.*

water studies

A Japanese doctor has conducted and published a series of experiments on what happens to water molecules when certain sounds are played to it. The results are astonishing. Water totally fragments, darkens or clouds over when loud, brash, unsynchronized sounds are played. This also happens when someone shouts angry, harsh words to it. When spoken to endearingly, or when classical music is played, the particles shine clearly, and rearrange themselves into the most beautiful patterns. Since our bodies contain up to 75 per cent water, it is not difficult to imagine that this is happening within us as we interact in our daily lives. What we listen to and how we speak therefore has a far-reaching effect on those that hear it. Your voice is soothing and calming when soft, that is why you instinctively lower your voice when chatting and murmuring sweet nothings to your baby. Your voice is one of your natural soothing and healing tools.

talking to your baby

The fact that she doesn't understand everything you say to her does not reduce the value of your spoken communication – her excited reaction confirms that she loves you talking to her. Chat to her during feeding, changing, when taking her somewhere by car – indeed, when you are doing anything at all. Use spontaneously exaggerated variable tones and facial expressions when speaking to your baby, in a way that you don't when talking to an older child or adult. Known as 'parentese', this dramatic sing-song pattern of spoken communication will grab your baby's interest.

sounds to lull your baby

The most calming sounds for babies are usually of a monotonous, regular and repetitive rhythm. Household background noises, such as the whirring drone of a dishwasher or washing machine, a distant vacuum cleaner or the ticking of a clock will draw your baby in and block out other family noises.

All of these sounds are just as effective if recorded and played back. CDs of running water or music intended to accompany meditation can help lull your baby to sleep, and classical music can have a calming effect (the Mozart effect). Alternatively, you could record a quiet drumbeat of between 60 and 70 beats per minute, which is similar to the human heartbeat.

Try to play a range of music to your baby so that she hears different musical instruments and tunes played at various speeds and rhythms, or use musical mobiles and toys, bells and rattles.

Your baby was used to hearing all sorts of sounds while inside your womb. If you can remember what you did to soothe yourself when you were pregnant, such as listening to a certain piece of music or watching a particular television programme, then he will probably be relaxed by the same music or theme tune. This imprint can be a useful tool when babies are upset, because they have already been conditioned to know that a particular sound equals a relaxed state.

TOO MUCH SOUND STIMULATION

For many adults it is difficult to tune out excess sounds. They cannot read a book if the television or radio is on. This kind of overload is felt by babies too. Therefore, when you are playing with, feeding or massaging babies, there should be no distracting sounds in the background.

touch

Inside the womb, touch is the first sense to develop, and once born a baby who is not touched will weaken and withdraw. Touch tells your baby that he is loved and safe, and it increases the flow of nutrient-rich blood that carries painkilling hormones through the body.

Above *Babies touch in order to explore and make sense of the world. It teaches them about themselves and the people that surround them.*

The human body contains thousands of touch receptors, many that we are not consciously aware of. If we constantly felt our clothes against our skin, for example, we would be driven to remain naked. These kinds of receptors switch off automatically, unless there is a problem. Remember, however, that a baby has to develop this awareness before his body's automatic system can learn to fine-tune it.

touch and memory

Babies develop their memory and sight alongside touch. Although his limbs are not making coordinated movements in the first month or so, when he touches something the touch receptors send information back to his brain. Through this process he begins to learn about objects and his body, remembering the sensations that are pleasurable and those that aren't. With the memory of this he will start to anticipate, so he gets excited when he sees your familiar face screwing up to give him a tummy raspberry. Likewise, he remembers that having something pulled up over his arms, neck and head was not a nice feeling, so he cries in advance as you begin to remove his clothes.

Touch is fundamental to teaching your baby about himself, his shape, his movement ability, his safety space, the people that surround him and the world that he now lives in. As soon as he can touch something his tiny fingers will automatically wrap around it as he feels it, in order to store this information for a later date.

touching with the mouth

Babies try to put things into their mouths as soon as they are physically able to. Through chewing and exploring an object with his mouth he can find out what it is, and will remember it when he puts it in his mouth again. Studies have shown that babies can visually recognize shaped objects after 'mouthing' them.

Left Your baby will get excited when he sees your face screwing up to give him a tummy raspberry because his memory has stored the sensation and the expression on your face.

Below Premature babies and newborns feel more secure – and benefit from – womb-like swaddling.

the touch-stimulated baby

A baby who does not like to be touched can be more difficult to bond with, due to the lack of cuddles and closeness. His touch receptors can be so sensitive that they receive far too much touch stimuli for him to cope with, and everything feels uncomfortable. Try not to move a touch-stimulated baby suddenly, and be especially gentle when changing him – don't change his clothes too often. Swaddling (see page 31) recreates a womb-like feeling that is comforting for touch-stimulated babies. Alternatively, lie a naked touch-sensitive baby in a warm room on a sheepskin rug and the softness will soothe him and placate his skin, and help to make him feel safe. These babies can be overstimulated and upset quickly by a small amount of touch and motion, and may not like to be rocked. A baby that does not like to be touched can gradually change with lots of gentle, loving care, time and tenderness.

Babies who are especially stimulated by touch (often premature babies) can grow into children who learn best by actually doing rather than listening or watching. They will learn by their mistakes.

the power of touch

It has been said that touch is the first and most fundamental form of all communication. Gentle touch communicates to the receiver's mind, body and spirit that we care about them. Every other sense has an organ to focus on, but touch is an all-over and all-consuming sensation.

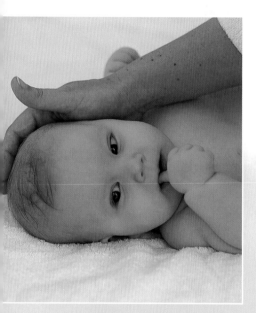

Above *The sensations of pain or pleasure can travel all over the body as the skin has thousands of touch receptors. By touching your baby she can feel how much you love her.*

Science has agreed that gentle touch is therapeutic and that touch can improve a person's well-being. Holding the hand of someone who is ill soothes them and gives them an emotional lifeline. Monitoring the heart rate of a person stroking an animal has shown that during the process blood pressure decreases, respiration improves as breathing deepens, circulation flows strongly and natural hormones are released inducing a feeling of contentment. Just being touched and cuddled will help a child to feel calm, nourished and secure.

why touch is important

Your baby learns a lot about the world around her through all the new sensations of temperature, pressure and texture. As you handle your baby, stroking, swaying, rocking and cuddling, you are getting to know each other in a unique way, since touch is in some ways the most direct language between people.

Studies show the effect of touch on babies to be manifold, and to persist long into their formative years. Massaged babies gain weight up to 50 per cent faster than unmassaged babies. They are more alert, active and responsive. They are more aware of their surroundings, better able to tolerate noise and are less likely to cry. When a mother and baby make plenty of physical contact, the mother gives emotional confidence and reassurance to her child.

There is a marked lack of physical and psychological growth when there is no touch in a person's life, and absence of touch in any age group leads to sickness and withdrawal. Many animal experiments have shown that even when the young are fed and can see their parents, when they are not touched they experience adverse changes in their heart rate, body temperature, brainwaves, sleep patterns and immune systems. Touching your baby expresses your love for her and enhances your relationship with her from an early age.

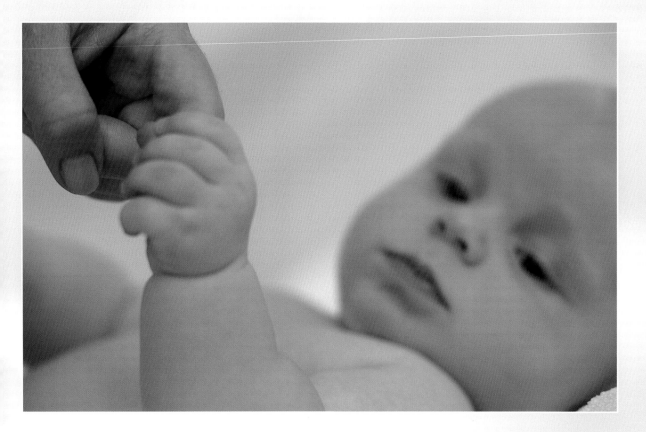

healing hands

A loving touch is stronger than a verbal communication of the same emotion. It can tell the body that it is loved at that moment in a more permanent way than the best poet in the world could express. Everyone has hands that give healing, whether consciously or not. The first thing a mother does when her child falls over is to offer to rub it better – if someone is in emotional pain, you offer a hug, you use your hands to give. Holistic healers concentrate on feeling and becoming aware of that sensation of giving love through the hands, and when they do this they can affect the receiver's mental, emotional, physical or spiritual wellness.

developing your sensitivity

Our hands are extremely sensitive – instruments of communication with which you can show your baby that you care. To make your hands more sensitive hold them 2 cm (1 in) apart for 30 seconds, then slowly draw them apart and push them close again, keeping all your attention on your palms. Repeat until your hands become warmer or tingle.

Above *The most immediate way to affect another person's well-being and to connect with them is to touch them.*

BACK PATTING
Gentle, rhythmic back patting can be very soothing for a baby. In many tribal cultures it is common to softly pat the whole body as a method of relieving stress.

complementary therapies and massage

herbal medicine

Herbs have been used for medicinal purposes for thousands of years, and herbal medicine uses plants and their chemicals to support the body's own efforts to defend itself from disease. You can soothe your baby by using herbal medicine to treat her discomfort, although check first with a registered medical herbal practitioner.

Above Herbal teas can either calm or stimulate you, depending on which herbs they contain. It is important to remember this if you are breastfeeding your baby, as it may be passed on in your breast-milk.

treatment

Always consult a qualified, registered herbal practitioner before you give your child any herbal medicines. The prescribed herbs can be taken internally, either brewed in boiling water to make teas, soaked in an alcohol medium that extracts the medicinal properties of the herbs to make tinctures, or as tablets, capsules, powders and juices. They can also be applied to the body externally as creams, ointments or poultices – herbs mixed with a liquid or oil that is placed on the body and covered with bandages – or added to your baby's bath.

Some of the causes of a baby's dis-ease which can be alleviated with herbal medicine include colic, constipation and diarrhoea, colds, coughs and breathing problems, cradle cap, eczema and nappy rash, teething pain, earache, conjunctivitus and sleep problems.

how to make a mild herbal tea

Combine 1 teaspoon of mixed herbs with a cup of filtered boiling water. Steep the herbs in the water for 5–10 minutes. Strain and leave to cool. For a baby weighing 2–12 kg (5–25 lb) a dose of 1–4 tablespoons several times a day is usual, but always follow the advice of your qualified practitioner.

how to take a herbal tincture

A few drops of tincture are usually taken in a little water. Evaporate the alcohol content of a tincture by pouring 1 teaspoon or more of boiling water directly onto the tincture in a cup, and leaving it uncovered for 10 minutes. For a baby the usual dosage is 2 drops for every 3 kg (7 lb) of her weight, but always follow your practitioner's instructions.

breastfeeding

If you are breastfeeding you can take an adult dose of the recommended tea or tincture, which will be transferred to your baby in a much smaller

Left A herbal steaming bowl in the room with vaporize mucus, clearing the air antiseptically and naturally.

quantity through your breast-milk. The standard adult dose for a herbal tea is 3–4 cups a day, and for a tincture is 30–60 drops (1–2 ml) 3–4 times a day. As usual, you should follow your practitioner's advice.

useful herbs for babies

- **Aloe vera** for burns and eczema.
- **Calendula cream** for cradle cap and nappy rash.
- **Chamomile** has a wealth of applications. In particular, it is a good herb for fever, teething pain, sticky eyes, colic, nappy rash and sleeping problems.
- **Comfrey ointments,** like aloe vera, are good for burns and eczema.
- **Echinacea** is useful in treating coughs and colds and in soothing eczema.
- **Fennel** for colic, constipation and teething pain.
- **Lemon balm** in the bath or as an infusion is good for colic, coughs and colds and fever.
- **Mullein** for respiratory problems and earache.
- **Tea tree** for coughs and colds and in a massage oil for nappy rash.
- **Lavender** is a great all-round soother. Lavender flowers in a tea can help with eczema, and lavender essential oil can promote restful sleep and calm a fever.
- **Raspberry leaf** for diarrhoea and conjunctivitus.

HOW HERBAL MEDICINE CAN HELP YOU

Herbs can help a new mother to cope with the range of emotions that come with having a new baby in the family, and treat the aches and pains often experienced after childbirth. Bergamot essential oil is nature's antidepressant; lavender essential oil relieves stress and promotes relaxation; lemon balm is wonderful for relieving stress and stress-related digestive problems; lime blossom tea is a relaxant and good for tension headaches and tension-related insomnia; meadowsweet is a gentle pain reliever; peppermint is good for indigestion, flatulence and headaches; and burdock root, comfrey leaf, nettle and raspberry leaf in a tea can help to heal the perineum. Consult a qualified practitioner to find out how herbs can help you.

homoeopathy

Homoeopathy is a gentle healing system that works on the principle that 'like cures like'. Homoeopathic remedies stimulate the body's own healing abilities to drive out the illness, and homoeopathy also boosts general well-being. It is suitable for the young and old, and is both effective and safe.

Above *Herbs and natural rememdies can help a new parent cope with the range of feelings and emotions that come with having a new addition to the family.*

treatment

Homoeopathy is a system of medicine that is holistic – that is, it takes into account mental, physical and emotional states. Homoeopathy can stimulate a baby's immune system, but you should always seek professional advice and treatment from a qualified homoeopath.

Homoeopathy has been used since the time of the early Greek civilizations, but it was 200 years ago that research undertaken by a German scholar and chemist, Samuel Hahnemann, evolved it to what we know today as homoeopathy.

Homoeopathy works on the principle of 'like treats like'. For example, an onion can cause a runny nose and a stinging and watering of the eyes, but if given the remedy *Allium cepa*, made from onion, these symptoms can be treated. You may therefore find *Allium cepa* helpful if you have a cold, hayfever or an allergic response.

The potency of homoeopathic remedies varies due to their dilution – they are diluted many times and shaken vigorously in between each dilution. For home use, a potency of 6, 12 or 30 is generally recommended, and you may need to take a 6 potency more often than a 30, as it will be more diluted.

These remedies are suitable for all, from young to old, and are recognized as safe and effective. They are taken in a tiny pill form, preferably without food or drink, and are best stored in their original containers away from direct sunlight and strong-smelling substances.

common homoeopathic remedies for baby

- **Arnica** for bruising.
- **Belladonna** for sore throats, earaches, eye inflammation and fever.
- **Bryonia** for constipation.
- **Chamomilla** for teething and earache.
- **Pulsatilla** for colds and coughs and whiney, clingy babies.

craniosacral therapy

Craniosacral therapy is a very gentle yet powerful tension-releasing therapy. At the core of the body the cerebrospinal fluid, which bathes and cushions the brain and spinal cord, moves in a tide-like ebb and flow, while bones, organs and other structures in the body follow in their own subtle way. Any unresolved tension is held in the body's tissues.

In the 1930s, the American osteopath William Garner Sutherland discovered that by gently manipulating the skull he could alter the flow of the cerebrospinal fluid, which in turn could help stimulate the body's ability to self-heal and help cure conditions not necessarily directly related to the cranium.

Above *Craniosacral therapy can invoke feelings of intense well-being in your baby.*

treatment

Craniosacral therapy can only be given by a qualified professional therapist. It is a specialist technique used to manipulate the bones of the skull with an extremely light touch, that for some people can barely be felt. The craniosacral therapist can feel the restrictions within the body's internal flow, and using the hands gently guides the body to let go of them. This therapy influences the muscular, skeletal, nervous, cardiovascular and immune systems, as well as the organs, connective tissue and fluids.

Some of the common causes of discomfort that can be soothed by craniosacral therapy include sleep problems, colic and digestive disturbances.

how craniosacral therapy can soothe your baby

Your baby's passage into the birth canal was like an intense massage, with crushing, gripping, twisting and thrusting movements. Common newborn problems, such as colic and suckling difficulties, may be due to the compression experienced during childbirth. If your baby constantly cries he could be holding tension anywhere in his body, while feeding difficulties may be due to tension that restricts his neck mobility.

Craniosacral treatments give a peaceful, reassuring awakening to your baby, during which time his system can release the tensions, stresses, strains and blockages held within the tissues, allowing a better flow of liquids and resulting in a much happier baby.

HOW CRANIOSACRAL THERAPY CAN HELP

Your body has been through massive, intense changes over the last nine months, culminating in the birth. Craniosacral therapy can help you to get over the physical trauma of this and make your back feel stronger again.

A single treatment may also help with any emotional disturbances, including postnatal depression.

aromatherapy

Throughout history and all over the world fragrant plants have been used in various ways to soothe, calm and heal. Aromatherapy uses the essential oils extracted from plant sources, diluted in various ways, to alleviate specific symptoms as well as to promote relaxation and well-being.

Right *All essential oils need to be mixed with a carrier oil, such as almond oil, before they are used.*

HOW AROMATHERAPY CAN HELP YOU

An aromatherapy treatment – some practitioners will visit you at home – can help with postnatal depression, relaxation, relieving stress and fatigue, as well as treating post-delivery aches and pains. Lavender and chamomile can soothe sore stitches and mastitis, and lavender can be applied topically to cracked nipples. Clary sage, bergamot and jasmine can help to relieve stress, and caraway, aniseed and verbena oils massaged on the breasts can encourage milk.

essential oils

Essential oils should not be used within the first 24 hours of birth, and if your baby was premature you should not use them until she has reached her original estimated birthdate.

The scent of essential oils can be imparted into a baby's room through a room spray, in a diffuser – 1 drop of oil to 1 dessertspoon of water – in a bowl of steaming water – 1–3 drops of oil to 600 ml (1 pint) water – or on a light bulb ring – 1 or 2 drops only. A single drop of oil can be diluted in a little milk and added to her bath. Essential oils can also be mixed with a carrier oil for massage, although this is not recommended for babies under three months of age. Essential oils are always diluted and a very low dosage is required for babies, usually 1 drop of essential oil to 15 ml of carrier oil, since their bodies are so small. Two mild oils most often advised for use with babies are lavender and Roman chamomile, both of which are particularly calming. Always carry out a patch test of the diluted oil before use (see page 84).

treatment

Aromatherapy massage with lavender or Roman chamomile essential oils can be carried out at home, as long as you keep to the 1 drop essential oil to 15 ml carrier oil ratio. For specific illnesses or concerns you should take the advice of a qualified aromatherapist. Aromatherapy oils can be used to ease the discomfort of teething problems, colds, colic, constipation, diarrhoea, nappy rash and dry skin, and to encourage deep sleep.

crystals

Crystals were used by many ancient cultures for healing and protection. They are thought to create a vibration that affects, balances and enhances our lives, to cheer you up, calm you down, motivate or uplift you and clear an atmosphere of general negativity.

choosing a crystal

The wonderful thing about choosing a crystal is that you can allow your instinct to make the choice. While certain crystals do have specific properties, you do not need to study a book to learn the effects of particular crystals. People tend to intuitively pick up the most appropriate one.

cleansing your crystal

Crystals need to be cleansed once you get them home, and at least once a month after that. For most crystals, run them under cold water, preferably rain water, to purify them. Other cleansing methods include passing the crystal through the smoke of incense or burning a herb, such as white sage.

Above Most crystals benefit from being placed on earth, then cleansed in cold water, before using. Some, however, do not tolerate water, so check when you purchase them.

how to use a crystal to soothe your baby

A crystal can be programmed to keep your baby safe and healthy or to soothe her. Simply hold the crystal in the palm of your hand and let your thoughts be heard. You may also want to dedicate it to the utmost good of all. Then place the crystal in the same room as your baby.

In the nursery, the crystal should be placed at least 1 m (3 ft) away from the cot, since it can energize your baby. If she is not settling with a crystal in her sleeping area, she may be being overstimulated by it.

HOW CRYSTALS CAN HELP YOU

You can choose a crystal for yourself in the same way as you choose one for your baby, based on instinct. You can carry it on your person, perhaps on a piece of jewellery, sleep with a calming crystal, or meditate with it. You will not necessarily always choose the same crystal, because you may feel differently each day. If you would like a bit of guidance, crystals do have certain associations which may influence your choice.

- Amazonite to be true to unconditional loving.
- Amethyst for divine connection.
- Aventurine for good luck.
- Celestite is calming.
- Clear quartz brings balance.
- Lepidolite is for harmony.
- Rose quartz is for nurturing and love.
- Ruby gives you energy.
- Smoky quartz helps to keep you focussed and grounded.
- Tourmaline for peace.

reflexology

Reflexology successfully treats and alleviates many illnesses and dis-eases. It is a form of foot massage: the right foot represents the right side of the body and the left foot the left side of the body. All the organs of the body have a particular corresponding reflex point on the foot, therefore it is possible to treat the whole body through the feet alone.

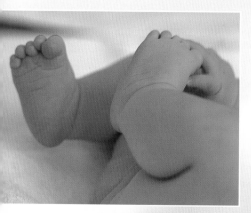

Above Tiny feet can be therapeutically massaged in minutes. Your baby's feet can either be bare or you can keep their socks on.

how is it done?

Working with the premise that energy runs through the body and pressure applied at certain points on the foot will unblock any stagnant or blocked energy in the body, the reflexologist works with gentle finger pressure only. The foot has been mapped out into five zones that run horizontally plus three vertical divisions, representing the areas above the shoulder, beneath the shoulder to above the waist and below the waist. If, when the reflexologist gently presses on a foot reflex, the patient experiences some pain or discomfort, it signifies that the corresponding area of the body is not functioning at its optimum. This may simply mean that at that particular moment that part of the body was under stress and needs relaxing. A reflexologist will usually apply a variety of strokes and pressures to the feet, and although at times some mild discomfort may be experienced, the client will normally feel a sense of well-being, as if they are walking on air by the end of their session.

Reflexology boosts the immune system and relaxes the whole body, creating the right conditions for the body to balance itself and commence self-healing. It is a holistic therapy, meaning that it treats the whole body (not just the symptoms) and relies on the body's self-healing process. It is also a preventative measure that can be used to keep you in good health, as well as for pure relaxation.

treatment

A qualified reflexologist will be able to find any discomfort in your baby's body that is causing him distress by gently massaging his feet. The therapy will be able to help with many of the problems that may be causing your baby's unrest, such as a runny nose or ear problems, colic, teething pain, constipation and diarrhoea, and asthma and eczema. By massaging your baby's feet you will be able to affect their sleeping patterns, alleviate symptoms of minor ailments and give your baby a sense of contentment.

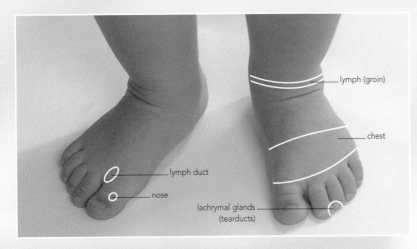

Left *It is not only the soles of the feet that contain areas sensitive to reflexology: they can also be found on the top of the feet and on the ankles.*

Below *Refer to the diagrams below for the positioning of the common reflexology points on your baby's feet.*

lymph (groin)

chest

lymph duct

nose

lachrymal glands (tearducts)

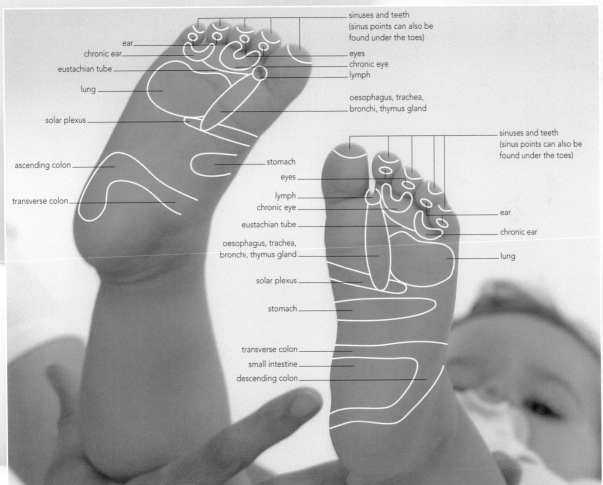

sinuses and teeth (sinus points can also be found under the toes)

ear

chronic ear

eustachian tube

lung

solar plexus

eyes

chronic eye

lymph

oesophagus, trachea, bronchi, thymus gland

ascending colon

stomach

transverse colon

sinuses and teeth (sinus points can also be found under the toes)

eyes

lymph

chronic eye

eustachian tube

oesophagus, trachea, bronchi, thymus gland

ear

chronic ear

lung

solar plexus

stomach

transverse colon

small intestine

descending colon

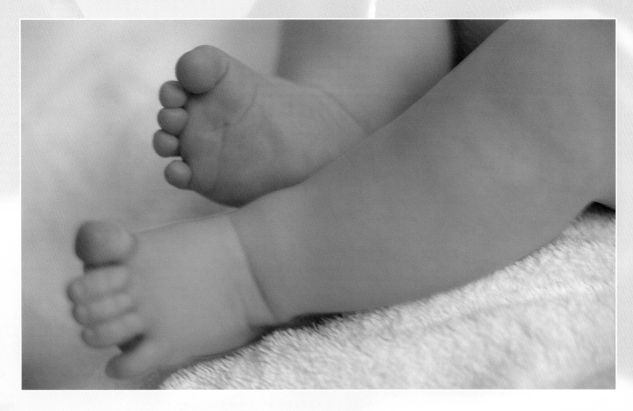

Above Some babies love having their feet rubbed, and find it very soothing, so use the principles of reflexology to give your baby a health-promoting ten-minute foot massage.

HOW REFLEXOLOGY CAN HELP YOU

A reflexology treatment could help with any back pain experienced after childbirth, is useful for breastfeeding problems and constipation and can also help to rebalance your hormones.

home treatment

This is a useful technique to try if your baby won't let you massage her whole body. Give each foot a five-minute massage, if possible once a day. Unlike body massage, your baby can keep most of her clothes on, which is great for the newborn who dislikes being naked. Make sure your baby is not too hot or too cold after a reflexology massage, since his temperature can be affected by it, and never massage if he already has a temperature. Make sure that she has lots to drink before and after the massage.

Don't be alarmed if the symptoms of illness become worse after a treatment of home reflexology massages. For example, skin problems can flare up for a couple of days, prior to improvement, and babies with sinus or mucus problems may have even runnier noses as the congestion clears.

A baby with colic will probably resist your pressure, no matter how light, on the stomach area of her foot, or start to cry, since it will feel uncomfortable. Where there is an area of concern in the body, the corresponding reflex may be sensitive, and if it becomes too difficult to touch, try holding and letting the heat of your hand relax that part of the foot. But if your baby has a serious condition always refer to your doctor.

a reflexology massage

Always begin by rubbing your hands together to warm them up. There is no need to use oils for this massage. Remember to make the massage a fun time and keep talking to your baby, chatting and cooing lovingly.

You will need to hold the foot at the heel for much of the massage, using your other hand to carry out the strokes. Keep your stroke soft, under no circumstances give anything more than a light touch at any time, since his feet will be very responsive. Babies will often make involuntary jerky movements and pull their feet away if your strokes tickle.

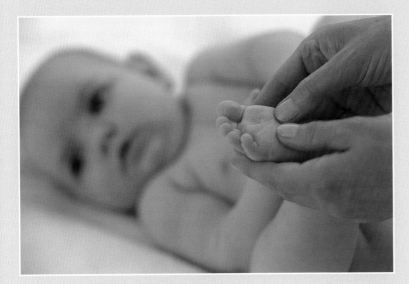

1 *Lay your baby on a towel or on your lap. If she is naked, make sure that the room is warm. Starting from the centre of the foot, use both hands to thumb stroke outwards covering the solar plexus. This relaxes your baby, releases tension, and will also deepen her breathing and aid digestion.*

2 *Hold her toes in one hand and use the other hand to gently rub the inside and outside of the heel area. This movement is good for releasing tension in the hips and abdomen, and especially useful for trapped wind.*

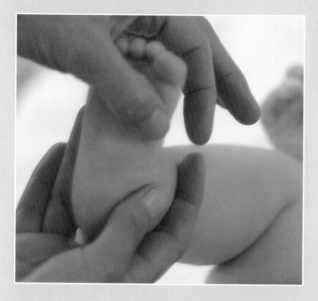

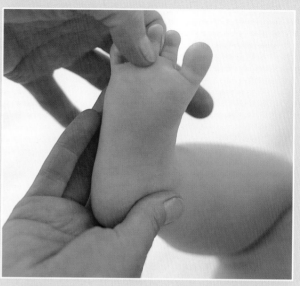

3 Finger stroke or make little circles from his heel to his big toe, moving along the instep and back again. Repeat two or three times. This movement relates to and relaxes the nervous system.

4 Make small circles where the toes meet the sole of the foot, from the little toe to the big toe and back again. This area relates to the sinus.

5 Recite the words and actions of This Little Piggy Went To Market on his toes, once only. This action relates to his ears and eyes, the cranial nerves, tissues and bones of the skull and teeth.

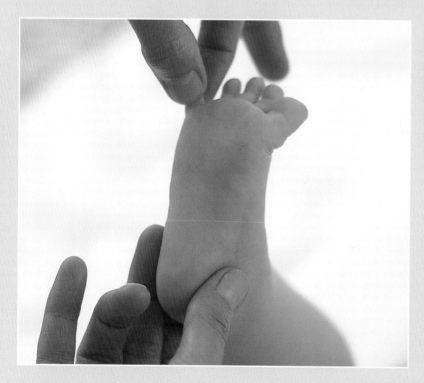

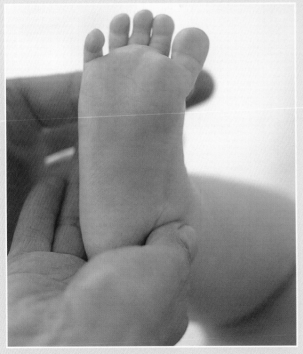

6 Softly stroke the top of his foot towards his toes to encourage lymphatic drainage. Tap gently over the top of his foot, which relates to the chest and releases mucus.

7 Firstly, stroke the top of his foot from his toes towards his ankle, encouraging his toes to open up. Then on the sole of the foot, stroke smoothly from the toes to the middle of the foot. His toes will curl under, exercising the muscles and bringing fresh, warming blood to that area to improve circulation. Repeat the whole routine on the second foot.

why massage?

Massage can soothe your baby in a multitude of ways. As well as relieving the discomfort or pain of a specific problem that may be unsettling her, massage makes a baby feel loved and secure. It can boost the immune system and improve circulation, and establishes a non-verbal form of communication between parent and child.

Above *Your baby's wellbeing and sense of being nurtured will always be enhanced by a loving touch, allowing deep bonding to take place.*

how massage can help your baby

Massage can have a very positive effect on the most common causes of a baby's unrest. Here are some of the different ways that you can use massage to soothe your baby.

to alleviate digestive problems, including colic and constipation

Babies are born with an under-functioning digestive system. It takes up to three months for them to fully develop the muscles involved in digesting food, which may account for the disappearance of colic at around that time. Premature babies often have colic because their digestive system is even more underdeveloped. Muscle tightness contributes to the gastro-intestinal difficulties, and this abdominal tension can cause wind to get trapped. Massage helps to relax the muscles, simultaneously toning and developing them, and allows the peristaltic movement of the colon to become stronger and more regular, thus alleviating constipation. When babies are born, the muscles needed for digestion are situated more to the back and sides of their bodies and massaging encourages them into their most efficient position.

to release muscle tension

Any form of muscle tension in a baby will create pain. Many handicapped babies experience frequent muscle spasms, which can be relieved with the aid of massage. Our bodies have the ability to release painkilling hormones called endorphins. Massage increases the flow of nutrient-rich red blood cells around the body, which releases and carries these natural painkillers. The slow, rhythmical stroking can soothe nerve endings, promoting comfort and easing tension and pain. The more you practise the massage, the more your hands become attuned to your baby, enabling you to give her extra holding or gentle stretching in areas of tension.

to ease teething pain

During teething babies often reach for their ear lobes. Interestingly, there is a pain-release point for the jaw, specified in acupuncture, in exactly this part of the ear. You can help by gently stroking the ears, jaw and gums, sedating the nerve endings and increasing the blood flow to assist easier presentation of the teeth.

as a feeding aid

Sometimes babies have trouble with the rooting reflex, especially premature babies. Massaging directly before a feed stimulates your baby's digestive system so that she is eager to feed and more enthusiastic about finding your nipple.

When it comes to weaning, the same process of massaging directly before the feed gives her body a heightened sense of hunger, so that eagerness to feed can overcome her sensitivity and reluctance to accept the bottle or food.

to regulate sleep patterns

Massage softens the muscles and allows more oxygen-enriched blood to flow around the body. This encourages deeper breathing and a better uptake of oxygen so that sleep becomes more inviting. The passive

Right Since babies spend so much of their time in a horizontal position blood flow to the extremities may be restricted. Massage will aid circulation and warm the baby's hands and feet.

HOW MASSAGE CAN HELP YOU

Massaging your baby can give a downhearted parent quality time with her new child. Gentle stroking and caressing, even just playing with your baby's feet, can stir caring mothering instincts to the surface, helping you to feel the needs of your baby. By watching your baby respond and move during the massage an interest and sensitivity can develop, leading to feelings of uselessness and inadequacy being replaced by a joyful desire to join with and discover your baby. Massage can encourage the changeover to motherhood, its warmth and intimacy overpowering desperation, duty and negativity. Once you can see and feel your baby responding to you in a positive way, you will feel more able to cope and, more importantly, you will want to.

workout of his muscles also leads to a restful state. Babies usually go into a deep, long sleep after massage, so it is best done before the night sleep.

to improve respiration

A baby will become fractious and miserable if a blocked nose causes minor breathing difficulties, particularly when it affects his sleep. During massage the oxygen uptake in the blood is increased and the extra stimulation for the immune system helps to deal with minor infections. Very gentle tapping over the chest also loosens any mucus.

to improve circulation

Babies often have cold feet or hands. This is partly due to the fast development of the internal organs and the demand this makes on the body's blood supply. Babies also spend a lot of their time in a horizontal position, so it can be difficult to get a good flow of blood to these parts. The increase in circulation during massage allows blood to flow easily around the body, carrying nutrients and oxygen to all the extremities. The nourishment in the blood promotes the increase of new cells and maintains a healthy supply of oxygen to the brain. As you massage you will notice how the feet and hands become warmer, and see your baby's whole body responding.

to improve skin condition

Your baby's skin is growing very quickly, and its texture can be helped by massaging with an organic almond or grapeseed oil, which nourishes and

feeds it. These oils are absorbed by the skin and do not block the pores. They moisturize and feed the skin, keeping it supple and encouraging the elimination of waste products known as toxins.

to boost the immune system

The lymphatic system is under-functioning from birth to approximately three months of age. Massaging stimulates lymphatic movement, thereby increasing the elimination of waste products that would otherwise build up and possibly create problems at a later date. This means that minor ailments, such as coughs or colds, can be more easily warded off, or at least not drag on for weeks on end.

Above *Massage helps foster trust and closeness for mother and baby.*

for muscle and bone development

Muscle and bone are fed with the nourishing blood that travels around our bodies. With strong bones and muscles your baby will be more coordinated with his limbs and hands. Once he is able to sit up and balance on his own, he will get great enjoyment and learning from his increased mobility and suppleness. Babies with disabilities can achieve an improvement in their muscle tone, stimulation and loving touch from the massage, which can be incorporated into their daily routine as something more enjoyable than any remedial work you may be having to do.

to help with bonding

Stroking massage can be done from the moment of birth, to facilitate the bonding process. By watching your baby's responses during the massage you share in a two-way communication with your baby, and vital emotional attachments can be forged. Massage also gives you the space and time to allow the bonding process to take place. An emotional bonding can be established, and stay, due to the awareness and communication now developing. Massage can develop trust and closeness for mother and baby.

before you begin

Massage is intuitive, but it will help to acquaint yourself with what you need to do before you begin. To ensure you both get the most out of this time, make sure you have everything you need close at hand, learn first about the strokes and a possible routine and communicate with your baby through your eyes and voice as well as touch.

Above *Remember to keep your essential oils in dark, airtight bottles in cool, dry places. Always replace the cap as they evaporate and blend them with your preferred choice of carrier oils.*

PATCH TEST

Before massaging, always place a little of the carrier oil (containing the diluted essential oil if you are using this) on your baby's ankle or wrist. A severe reaction would show within 30 minutes, but wait for 24 hours to eliminate any sensitivity. If there is any sign of irritation, do not use the oil.

carrier oils

Having some oil on your hands while massaging helps them to move smoothly and cleanly over your baby's body. Carrier oils are so-called because they usually 'carry' essential oils, which should never be applied neat to the skin. It is not necessary to use essential oils for massage, unless you have been advised to do so by a qualified aromatherapist. Carrier oils can be used directly on the skin, provided there is no allergy – always test the oil on a small area of skin on the wrist to check for a reaction (see box below left).

Mineral-based oils are not ideal for massage because they stay on top of the skin, blocking the pores. Instead vegetable oils such as grapeseed and almond are commonly used. Apricot is considered a hypo-allergenic oil that is very useful on sensitive skin. Grapeseed oil is quite thin and easily absorbed, while almond and apricot are a little thicker. Olive oil is also used in some cases – such as for cradle cap – because it is quite thick and highly nutritious. Avocado and jojoba are two other vegetable oils that are often used.

Since carrier oils are made from vegetable sources they can go off, so it is a good idea to buy them in small bottles. To prolong their life they should be stored in a cool, dark place.

getting ready

An ideal time for massage is in the early evening, before your baby's last feed, because the massage should promote deep, relaxing sleep.

Before you begin, gather everything you need around you. A sheepskin rug makes a wonderful mat as it is soft and helps to keep your baby warm. Alternatively a towel can be placed over a changing mat. You will also need some tissue or kitchen paper to wipe away any mess, cushions for your own comfort, a glass of water, your baby's bottle – or be ready to breastfeed since babies can get very hungry after massage – a clean nappy, a spare towel to wrap your baby in at the end, and a carrier oil.

Left *Do not constrict your baby in any way. If he wants to move around, let him, and enjoy his playfulness.*

Your baby can be massaged naked, if she is happy to be, or you can isolate parts of the body to work on and leave the rest still clothed.

Remove any jewellery and make sure your fingernails are not likely to scratch. Take the telephone off the hook and turn off the television. Play some soothing music if you like, but make sure it will not distract your attention from your baby. Dim the lights or draw the curtains if necessary to block out bright sunlight. Make sure your hands are warm – rub them together if needed. Put some oil in the palms of your hands and rub them together to make your hands softer and more receptive. Wiggle your fingers in front of her eyes, loosening your joints and getting her attention. Once you have followed on with the massage a few times your baby will get excited when she sees you doing this, as she remembers what is to follow.

things to remember

A full body massage takes about 20 minutes, but stop and start as you and your baby please. Every baby has a different tolerance level and attention span. When you sense your baby has had enough it is time to stop. If your baby does not appear to like a certain movement, or part of her body being touched, make a mental note to touch and hold that part as often as possible during your everyday routine. She is probably holding tension in that area, which can be released by your hand resting on those muscles.

Endearingly talk to your baby during the whole massage, allowing your voice and actions to be soft and gentle. A huge amount of communication happens with eye contact, so have as much as possible as you massage.

WHEN NOT TO MASSAGE

Under certain circumstances you should not massage your baby, due to illness or discomfort:
• If your baby is on medication, seek medical advice first.
• Pre-term babies have much more sensitive skin and often prefer skin-to-skin cuddles only.
• If your baby has a kidney problem.
• If your baby has a heart problem.
• If your baby suffers from epilepsy.
• If your baby has a high temperature.
• If your baby has high/low blood pressure.
• If your baby has unexplained rashes or spots (eczema can be aggravated, although not always).
• If your baby has any cuts, swellings, abrasions, sprains, bruising or broken bones.
• If your baby has recently been immunized.
• If your baby has loose or 'clicky hip' joints there are some movements you should leave out.
• Massage should never take place directly after a feed, as your baby's energy is then being used to digest and absorb all the nutrients. Ideally wait 1½ hours for the digestive process to be completed.

Preliminaries

Gather everything you need and make sure the answer machine is on. The room you use must be warm enough for your baby to feel comfortable without his clothes.

1 *Find a position to massage in that is comfortable for both you and your baby. Any tension in your body is transferred to your baby, so it is essential that you are supported and comfortable. Make sure the room is nice and warm and that you are not positioned in a draught.*

2 *Try sitting on the floor or laying your baby on a mat on a table so that you can sit on a chair or stand up. Pluck the shoulders to release the tension held in them from birth.*

3 You may like to lay or sit him on a towel on your lap, with your legs outstretched or bent up. In this position you are at a very good distance for your baby to be able to focus on your face.

4 Many babies who have not spent much time on their tummies love laying over your legs for their back massage.

a massage routine

Massage is made up of two simple, soft strokes. One is long, slow, slippery and smooth, to relax, and the other is slightly faster, to stimulate. Most movements can be repeated four or five times, or as your baby likes. You do not have to follow these movements in any particular order, or necessarily do them all.

This massage routine is meant as a guide only. To truly connect with your baby you need to follow your intuition and listen, through your hands, to what your baby is telling you. You do not have to complete a whole body massage every time, but be guided by your baby, and next time start where you left off, in order to cover the whole body.

front of body massage

This massage of the face and front of the body makes for a gentle introduction that naturally leads on to the rest of the body. Rub your hands together to warm them up and smooth oil into them. Remember to keep adding oil as you proceed through the massage and to look at your baby and softly talk to him throughout the routine.

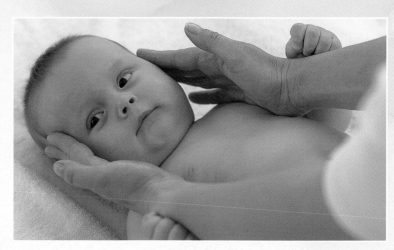

1 *Lay your baby on his back. Wave your fingers over his face to attract his attention and loosen and soften your finger joints.*

2 *Stroke your fingers out from the centre of his forehead and circle his temples a few times. Softly stroke both hands down to his jaw and down the side of his neck. Now thumb stroke with both hands from the edge of his nose to his jaw. This encourages lymphatic drainage.*

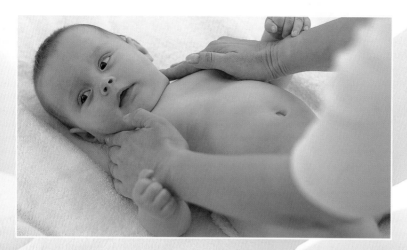

3 Slowly and lightly stroke over his shoulders and into his armpits, ensuring you have enough oil on your hands to easily slide over his body. Remember your hands will absorb the oil, according to how dry they are.

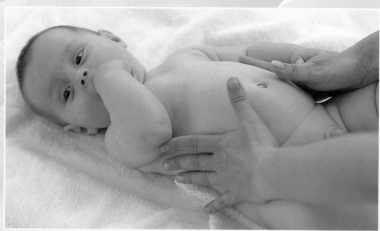

4 Continue the previous movement down his sides and then over the front of his body two or three times.

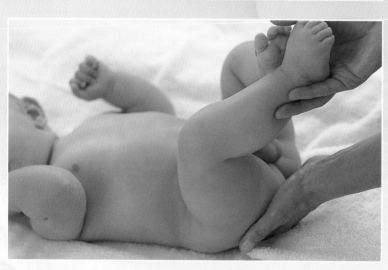

5 Hold his feet up with one hand and slide the other under his buttocks to the base of his spine. This area houses nerve endings to the digestive system and is an extremely soothing place to massage. Gently circle your fingers five or six times, asking your baby how that feels today.

leg massage

Remember to keep your hands oiled enough to slide easily over your
baby's legs, and to keep your baby's attention with your endearments.
To begin with, pass both hands over both of his legs, from his thighs
down to his toes. Now work on one leg at a time.

1 *Softly wrap your whole hand around
the top of his thigh and place your
other hand around the back of his
thigh. Drag and slide both hands down
to his ankle. Now, with the same hand
position, smoothly glide one hand after
the other from thigh to ankle. Do not
straighten or pull the leg. Make sure the
oil goes into the creases of his thigh.*

2 *Using your thumb or two
fingers gently make fast circular
movements up and down the inside
and outside of his leg twice. Try to
merge your fingers into the fleshiness
of the leg to stimulate the circulation.
Repeat Step 1.*

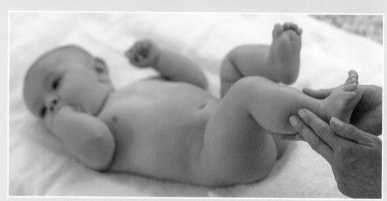

3 *Hold his ankle and cup your
other hand under his calf. Softly
and lightly squeeze up from his ankle
to the top of his thigh and down again,
working over his thigh and calf twice to
relax and tone the thigh muscles and
increase circulation. Repeat Step 1
before repeating the whole routine
on the second leg.*

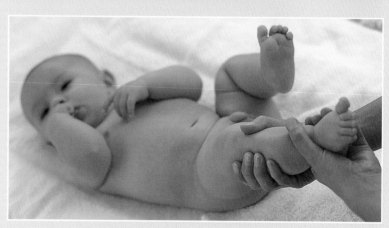

tummy and chest massage

Babies often cry as you place your hands on areas of discomfort. To comfort him, using those dulcet tones, keep chatting to your baby, telling him what it is that you are doing, and asking him if he likes it. Make sure your hands have enough oil on them to slide easily over your baby's skin.

1 *Slide one hand under his buttocks to the base of his spine, gently holding his feet up with the other hand. Make small circular movements, either clockwise or anticlockwise, trying to maintain eye contact. Come back to this movement if your baby starts to cry during the tummy massage.*

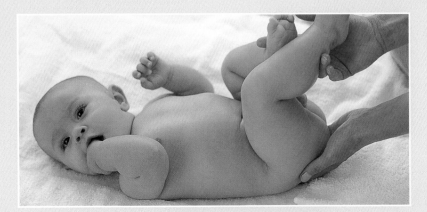

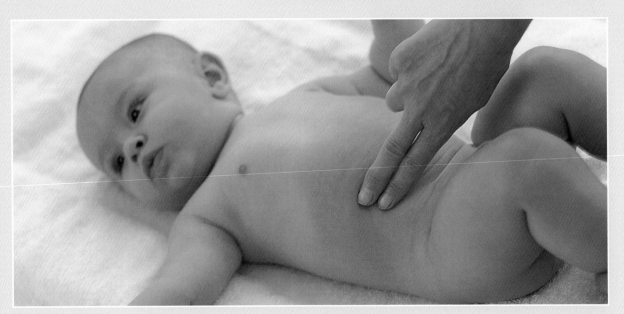

2 *Using two fingers, with no pressure, make tiny clockwise circles across his tummy, moving up from his right leg, across the body – above his belly button – and down towards his left leg. It is here that you may be able to feel, and soften up, any solidifying matter that is causing your baby discomfort or constipation.*

3 Spread your hand like a fan and mould your palm into the shape of his tummy. Make a long, slow, sweeping continuous circle over your baby's abdomen, with absolutely no pressure. Do this twice. Now gently drag one hand after the other from his side, under the last rib, towards his belly, working several times on each side.

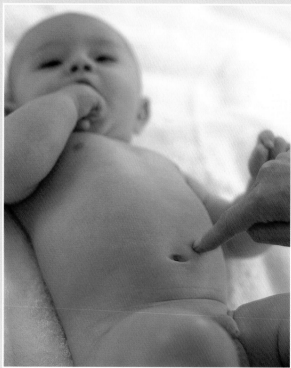

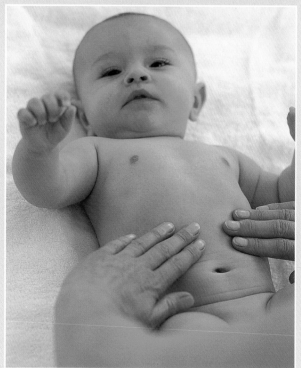

4 If your baby's belly button is protruding, include some small, slow fingertip circling movements around it but do not apply any pressure. This stimulates the muscles to encourage the belly button to recede.

5 Using both hands together, smoothly sweep out from the base of his sternum to his sides, following his ribcage as it curves out to the sides.

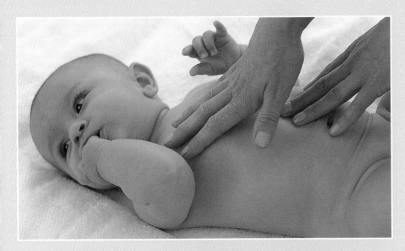

6 Let one hand, fingertips and palms, follow the other diagonally from the shoulder to the hip. Repeat on the other diagonal.

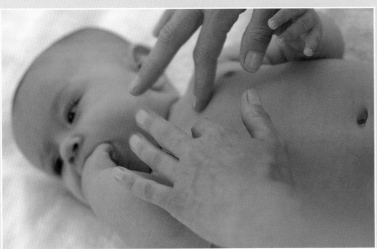

7 Lightly tap your fingers over your baby's chest. This will help to loosen any mucus and relieve any tension when they are chesty or have a cold. Remember your eye and voice connections.

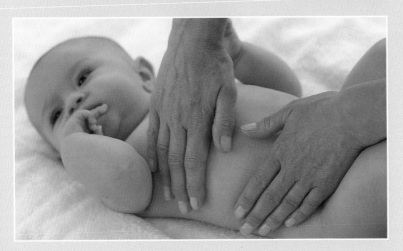

8 Place both hands on your baby's side and softly slide them apart so that one hand moves towards his hip and the other towards his armpit. Do not physically stretch your baby or his skin. Repeat on the other side.

shoulders and arms massage

Many babies cry when you start to massage their shoulders since this area can hold tension from birthing. Remember to lovingly speak to your baby and gaze into her eyes, if possible. Keep your hands nicely oiled so that they easily slide over her skin.

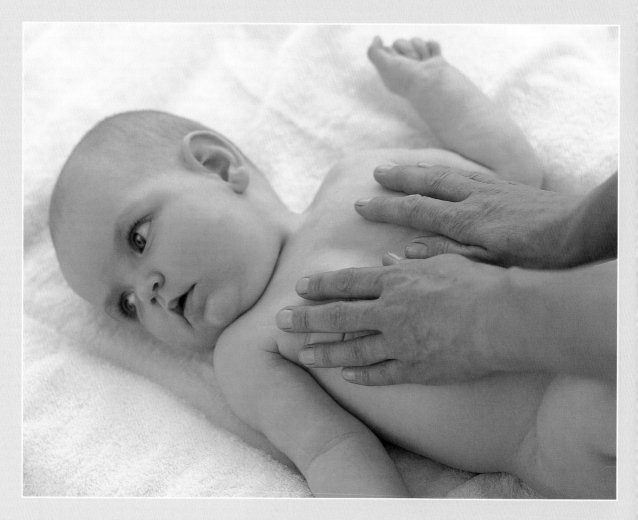

1 *Glide both hands up from your baby's tummy, over her shoulders and down her arms, relaxing her shoulder muscles and bringing relief to neck tension.*

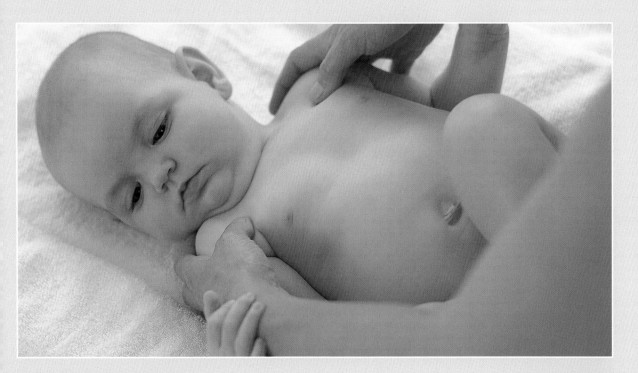

2 *Using both hands, stroke down her arms from her shoulders. Gently squeeze then stroke the arms, increasing the circulation and encouraging more movement and less tension. Gently pluck the shoulders. Keep cooing lovingly to reassure her, since your baby is likely to stiffen apprehensively at this instance. Do not try to force or straighten her arms – let her do this when she is ready.*

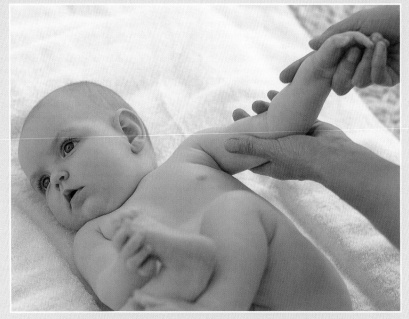

3 *Using both hands, stroke from her neck, over her shoulder to the top of one arm. Wrap your whole hand around the top of her arm and tenderly lift and glide your hand to her wrist, one hand flowing after the other.*

4 Bring her arm over her chest, but do not force any movement your baby does not like. Make small circles along the outside of the arm, then gently slide your hands towards her wrist. Slowly and gently open her arm out again, encouraging more flexibility and muscle alignment. Repeat Steps 3 and 4 on the other arm.

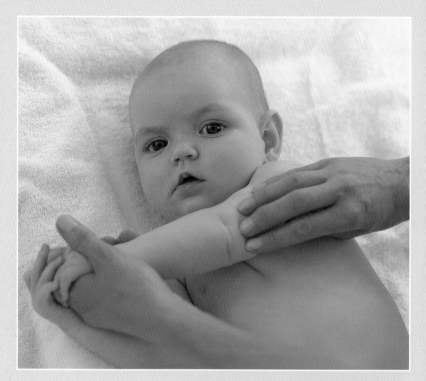

5 Lightly try to bring her hand to meet her opposite knee over her belly. Again, do not force any movement: only do as much as your baby is comfortable with.

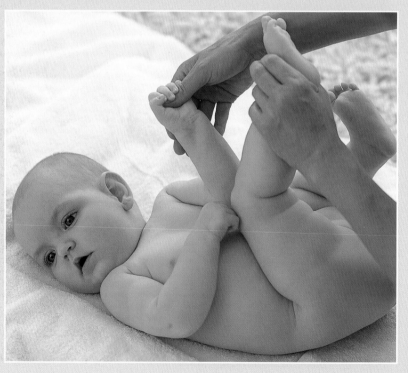

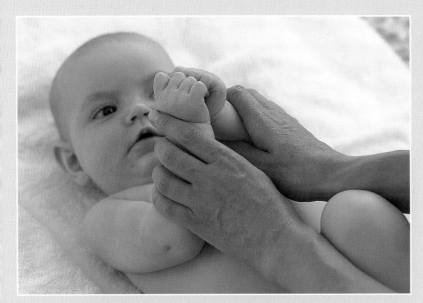

6 Clapping both her hands
together, recite a nursery rhyme,
stimulating her brain cells as she
begins to recognize and respond
to certain playful sounds.

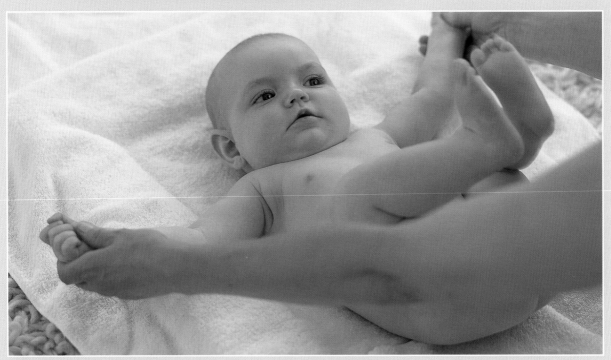

7 Slowly and gently open her arms wide and play peek-a-boo, really
loosening and relaxing her shoulder and upper arm tendons and
ligaments. Finish with long, smooth strokes of your palms up her arms,
down her body and up again, as though you are conducting an orchestra.

back massage

Lay your baby on his stomach. Let his arms be placed so that he can try to push himself up, bearing in mind that he will decide how he wants to lie. Keep murmuring sweet nothings to reassure him and have enough oil on your hands to sweep smoothly over his body.

1 *Sweep both hands all the way up his body, from his feet to his shoulders, and down again two or three times. Massage out to his sides, gently following his ribs. Tap over his upper back to loosen any mucus.*

2 *Using your thumbs, very gently make little circles all over his buttocks, moving from the centre out. This helps to relax and tone the muscles around the hip joint. Gently stroke out to his sides with your whole hands, moving up towards his shoulders.*

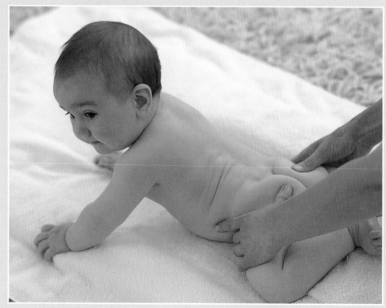

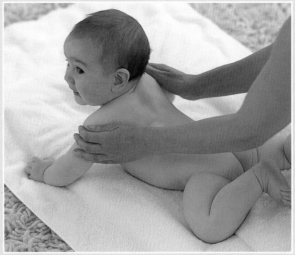

3 *Starting at the base of your baby's spine, use the back of your hands to stroke your fingers from his spine outwards, in a flowing movement. Repeat this movement working up towards his shoulders. Now use your palms to sweep down his back and up again.*

4 *Gently pluck at the fleshy top of his shoulder to ease tension. This can be a sensitive area, in need of tender caresses. With your fingertips, gently massage out from his spine towards his shoulders. Sweep over his arms and come back to his back. Sweep down to his buttocks and up again, in one continuous stroke.*

5 *Finish the back massage by gently and repeatedly stroking down either side of his spine, from the top to his buttocks. Let the stokes start with your whole hand and diminish to a few fingers, then one finger only, light as a feather.*

face massage

Most babies don't like having their face massaged for the first few times, but grow to love it. To comfort your baby chat lovingly to her or hum, sing or make one continual tone – a kind of sound massage that is nice to incorporate now as you are focussing on each other closely. Rub some oil into your hands so that they glide smoothly over her skin.

1 *Starting at the side of her nose, gently massage over her cheeks in circles, moving towards her jaw. This helps with lymphatic drainage and may relieve a blocked nose.*

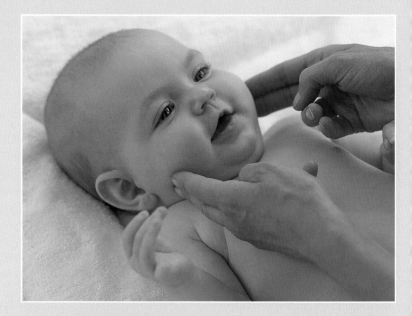

2 *Release and tone her jaw muscles with small circular movements over the cheeks above and along the jaw bone, using the side of your finger. This may help to relieve teething pain.*

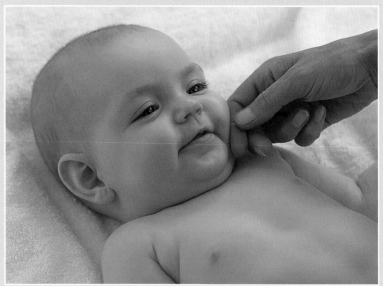

3 *Gently circle along the jaw and down the sides of the neck. This may help with the pain of teething.*

TEMPLE MASSAGE

Slowly and gently thumb stroke outwards over your baby's forehead to her temples. You may prefer to change your position so that you sit behind her head and look over her. Circle the temples three times and stroke down towards her jaw. Stroke over the top of her nose to the tip, with alternate fingers, to finish. This soothing temple massage will help to stimulate lymphatic drainage.

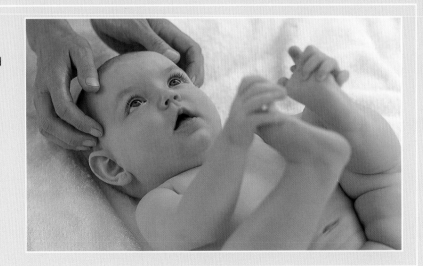

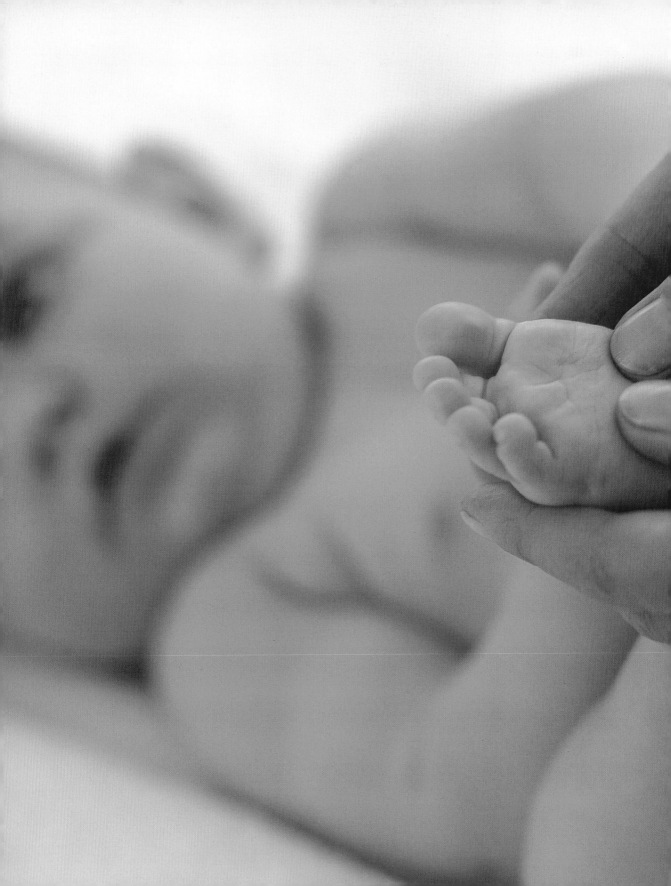

natural
remedies

digestive problems

A newborn baby's digestive system is not fully developed, which is why babies often have problems with wind, constipation and diarrhoea. Soothing your baby during these uncomfortable times involves a lot of holding, rocking and possibly massage, although there are complementary therapies that can also help.

Above *Some colicky babies respond to being held high over the shoulder. A gentle rub on the back and your soothing voice will also help.*

colic

If your newborn has colic it can make life extremely difficult for the whole family. A colicky baby will cry a lot at a particular time of day, usually in the early evening, and be difficult to comfort. Most believe colic is caused by trapped wind or stomach cramps caused by contractions in the colon, and it has also been related to unresolved cranial mouldings due to the birth conditions.

Whatever the cause, your baby can do nothing about it, and neither, it seems, can you. No matter what you try your baby still continues screaming, red-faced, stiff and upset. Colic can affect bonding and drain your emotions, since you feel desperately discouraged and distraught – you can't leave him to cry nor can you pacify him. It is important to remember, however, that your baby is having a harder time than you.

what you can do

It is a good idea to have someone else around to help during the worst times of the day. This should relieve some of the tension you are feeling – that in turn passes to your baby – due to worry and perhaps lack of sleep. The ideal support system here is family, bearing in mind how well you all get along. Failing that, however, good friends, neighbours, crèches and other mothers can provide essential support. Other people will be able to distance themselves from the problem, because they are not the mother and 24-hour carer, so, if their comforting works, do not compare yourself to them, making yourself feel inadequate on top of everything else.

While it is not a good idea to leave a baby to cry for long, since they begin to feel abandoned and get more discouraged, wretched and dispirited, there will be times when, for the sake of your sanity, you may have to do this. Lay your baby on a mat on the floor surrounded by cushions, or put him in his pram in the garden, and leave him for a few minutes, allowing yourself the time you need to calm down and regain

Left Many babies with colic like to be held in this position as their body weight creates enough pressure on their stomachs to move the trapped wind.

your composure and ability to cope with the crying.

Try using movement to soothe your baby by taking him out in the car or pushchair. The motion of travelling, coupled with the noise of the engine in a car can sometimes calm the fractious crying. Similarly, attaching your baby to your body in a sling has the same effect. This might seem inconvenient, but your smell, the movement and personal contact will help to calm him. Compared to lying down, in this position there is less pressure onto and into his tummy or back, and your movement allows his wind to disperse.

Experiment with different ways of holding your colicky baby to discover which one soothes him the most. Mothers usually find holding him high over the shoulder, as opposed to leaning him onto the shoulder, to be a comforting position. Some babies are also calmed by a warm bath with one of their parents.

Trapped wind is thought to be the cause of colic and is particularly uncomfortable and painful. A baby with trapped wind will try to draw his legs up towards his tummy. In this instance he should not be left to cry for long periods of time since crying can trap even more air. A regular rocking motion works well for minor wind, bringing him into an upright position and gently rubbing his back. Sometimes simply picking him up and walking around is the only option, holding him tenderly until the wind disperses itself. Speaking in low soft tones will help to keep you calm and also reassure him, while cycling and massaging his legs can dislodge some of the discomfort, as long as he doesn't have hip problems. Laying your

REMEMBER, IT WILL PASS

Colic can affect a baby from the first three weeks of birth. But it will disappear again after three months. So remember, if you need a positive outlook, that the nightly crying or screaming fits will come to an end, and that your child will give you a lifetime of pleasure.

HOW MASSAGE HELPS

By massaging directly before a feed, your baby's digestive system is stimulated so that he is eager to eat. You can also try massaging his feet while he is feeding.

Above *Keep trying different positions until you find the best one for your colicky baby.*

baby on his stomach over your arms or legs can sometimes give some relief and help to push the trapped air out.

Rocking can often soothe a colicky baby. Hold him close to your body, facing out, with his spine in close contact with your body. Slide your hand under his stomach to support him and rock in this position. Alternatively, lay him across your knees and rock yourself from side to side while gently bouncing your knees up and down.

Stroking his ear, accessing the acupuncture points there, can also soothe the crying.

If you are breastfeeding look at the foods you have eaten over the past 24 hours. You may want to avoid eating spicy foods, citrus and gassy foods such as beans and sugar, as foods that make you windy are likely to have the same effect on your baby. Try drinking chamomile, peppermint or fennel tea, or chewing cinnamon, since the calming properties of these herbs will pass through to your baby in your milk while tea or coffee will have a stimulating effect. Also make sure that you are drinking plenty of water.

massage for the colicky baby

Gently moving your baby's legs can bring him relief from trapped wind, however some leg movements should not be carried out if your baby has problems with his hips. The discomfort of most digestive problems can also be alleviated with this massage. Smooth some oil on to your hands and remember to look at your baby and talk to him throughout the massage.

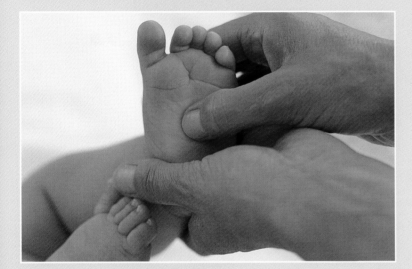

1 *Using your thumb or fingers, with no pressure, make little circles in the centre of his right foot, increasing to a bigger circle that encompasses the whole of the sole. Repeat on the other foot.*

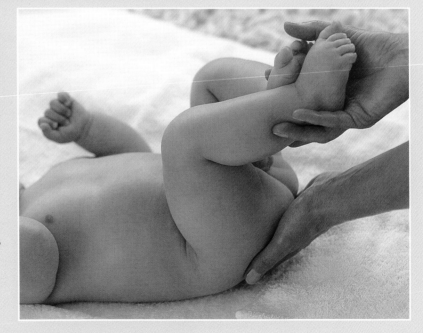

2 *Slide one hand under his buttocks to the base of his spine, gently holding his feet up with your other hand. Make small circular movements, either clockwise or anticlockwise. This area houses the nerve endings for the digestive system and is generally a very soothing place to massage.*

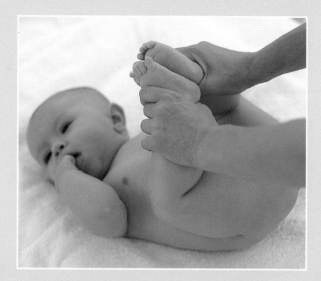

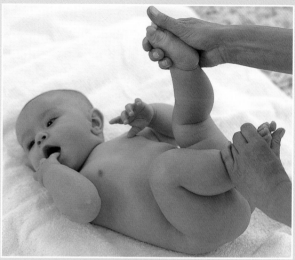

3 Omit this movement if you have any concerns about your baby's hips. Slightly bend both legs together, in towards the tummy. This is excellent for relieving wind. Make the movement as small or as big as your baby allows, but never force a movement.

4 You should also omit this movement if you have any concerns about your baby's hips. Bicycle his legs one way and then the other. Do not force the legs, but allow and encourage whatever movement he can manage. Accompanying this movement with a nursery rhyme will help to stimulate his brain. You will notice, if you repeat the same nursery rhymes each time you massage, that your baby responds and will start to gurgle in anticipation as you approach these parts of his massage.

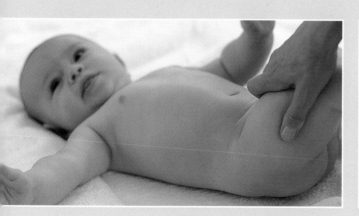

5 Gently squeeze his thighs with one hand. This movement encourages the release of tension from the muscular attachments that run through the abdomen.

6 Repeat the previous movement with both hands as you sweep down to the ankles.

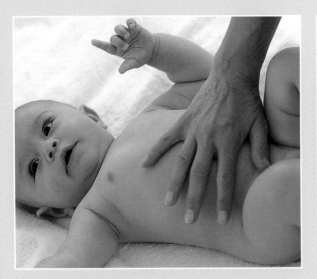

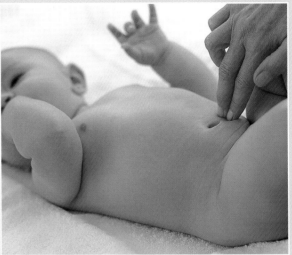

7 *This next movement needs to be done accurately, since it follows the colon in the direction of the exiting faeces. Make sure you have enough oil on your hands to easily glide over your baby's body. Work with the whole of your dominant hand, not just your fingers. Place your palm over his abdomen and make a large clockwise circle on his abdomen, around and above the navel. Do not press into his body, but form a slow, smooth, continuous circle. Give lots of reassurance.*

8 *With two fingers, make tiny circles on his abdomen, moving up from his right leg, across his body above the belly button and down towards his left leg. This follows the same direction and route over the colon as you have just covered with the palm of your hand. Repeat Steps 6 and 7 a few times. Practised regularly, this massage can be a preventative measure as well as an aid.*

complementary therapies that can help

- **Aromatherapy:** Massage (see above) with Roman chamomile essential oil, mixed to a ratio of 1 drop essential oil to 15 ml carrier oil, or use lavender essential oil mixed to the same ratio.
- **Craniosacral therapy:** consultation. Releasing the tension in the abdomen allows for better movement of trapped wind.
- **Herbal medicine:** consultation. Fennel or lemon balm teas may be prescribed, and chamomile, lemon balm and lime flowers added to the bath can also help.

- **Homoeopathy:** consultation. Chamomilla is suitable for a baby that likes to be held; Pulsatilla for a baby that likes to be rocked; Lycopodium for lots of wind; Dioscorea for a baby that likes to arch his back; and Mag. Phos. for a baby that is helped by a warm bath.
- **Reflexology:** consultation. Tension can be released in the stomach and muscular system through the feet, allowing trapped wind to escape.

healthy bowel functioning

Babies may sometimes not have a bowel movement for a couple of days in a row.
This may simply be part of a phase or it could also be constipation. However, if her
movements are starting to cause distress, then you can help with massage or with
other therapies.

Above *Massaging your baby's feet whilst*
feeding can help with any digestion problems.

constipation

Constipation – hard stools that are difficult to pass – is usually due to muscular tension, and/or an immature digestive system. Breastfed babies rarely suffer from constipation, but they may have phases of passing infrequent stools – up to four or five days is quite common – so do not worry unless the stools are hard or painful to pass. Bottle-fed babies are more prone to constipation, passing hard stools, and should be given more water to drink.

Constipation without illness is nothing to worry about so long as it does not last for long, but there are ways that you can ease the general discomfort of this condition as your baby may be more upset than normal.

what you can do

Massaging the stomach with a carrier oil can help to ease the tension in the muscles and relieve the discomfort (see pages 91–3).

complementary therapies that can help

- **Aromatherapy:** massage the colon (see page 109) with a lavender essential oil mix, 1 drop essential oil to 15 ml carrier oil.
- **Craniosacral therapy:** consultation.
- **Herbal medicine:** consultation. Dandelion, liquorice or flaxseed may be prescribed, along with water and prune juice.
- **Homoeopathy:** consultation. Alumina is suitable if the stools are soft but infrequent, especially in newborns; Bryonia if the stools are hard and dry and the baby is thirsty and grumpy; and Calcerea Carb. if the baby is contented and doesn't mind being constipated.
- **Reflexology:** consultation. Working over the bowel points can help regulate the peristaltic movements – the involuntary muscle movement that propels the contents of the alimentary canal – required for normal bowel functioning.

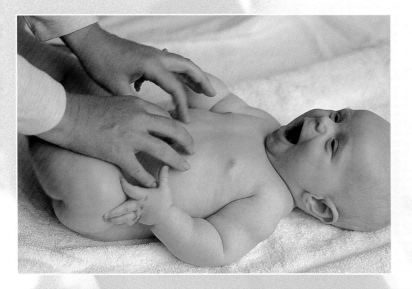

Above Playing with your baby and massaging their stomach and colon before a feed can ease tension so that they can feed in a more relaxed manner.

diarrhoea

Diarrhoea can be caused by a food intolerance, a bacterial or viral infection or teething. It is usually a short-term problem, but can cause your baby to become dehydrated, so allow for extra bottles or feeds on the breast. If the diarrhoea continues for more than a few hours, or is accompanied by vomiting, contact your doctor.

what you can do

Massaging the colon, base of the spine and feet with a carrier oil can help to relieve any discomfort (see page 109).

complementary therapies that can help

● **Aromatherapy:** massage (see page 109) with a Roman chamomile essential oil mix, 1 drop essential oil to 15 ml carrier oil.

● **Herbal medicine:** consultation. Carob powder, slippery elm or raspberry leaf may be prescribed, along with apples – because of the pectin – made into apple sauce for a baby who is taking solids.

● **Homoeopathy:** consultation. Arsenicum is suitable for a sweaty, restless and chilly baby, and for stomach bugs or food poisoning; Colocynthias if the diarrhoea is accompanied by cramps and doubling over; and phospherous for the baby who is thirsty, tired and has watery stools.

● **Reflexology:** consultation. The reflexologist will work over the bowel points to bring back normal functioning. You can help by gently massaging the base of the heel and the centre of the sole.

NEW FOODS

As you wean your baby on to solid foods, don't forget that her stools and bowel movements will change. If her stools become very loose and watery after introducing a new fruit or vegetable, don't give her that food again for several days, then reintroduce it in a small quantity.

skin irritations

*Skin irritations are common, and usually cause only minor discomfort. However, some
can be caused by allergic reactions to chemicals used in soaps, shampoos and powders,
so avoid artificially scented, chemical-based oils and lotions. If you are breastfeeding,
your baby may have had an allergic reaction to something you have eaten.*

Above *Gently massage olive oil into your
baby's scalp. This thick wax drains away into
their lymphatic system, so follow on with the
facial massage to keep clearing her lymphatics.*

cradle cap

This scalp complaint is extremely common and does not signify eczema
in later life. The greasy yellow scales on the scalp do not itch, and while
unpleasant to look at, it is not a serious condition. Although the cause of
cradle cap is not clear, some suggest it may be a fungal infection. What is
evident, however, is that it is not the result of bad hygiene. Cradle cap can
appear at any age between three to nine months and has usually gone
by the age of one year.

what you can do

Regular soft brushing will help to dispel the scales, but do not pull off
any crusts. Gently massage 2 drops of lavender essential oil in 50 ml of
olive oil into your baby's scalp at night, avoiding the fontanelle. This mix is
quite sticky and smelly, but extremely nutritious. Comb the flakes and oil
out with a fine-toothed comb in the morning then shampoo with a very
mild herbal shampoo.

complementary therapies that can help

● **Herbal medicine:** consultation. A calendula ointment may be prescribed
or an infusion of marigold to rinse your baby's scalp with.

dry skin

Dry skin is common in babies that have been induced or were overdue.

what you can do

Massage the affected areas with carrier oil or olive oil (see pages 86–99).

complementary therapies that can help

● **Aromatherapy:** massage the area with a lavender or German chamomile
essential oil mix, 1 drop essential oil to 15 ml carrier oil.

Above *Always use organic oils and lotions as well as shampoos and soaps where possible.*

eczema

There are several different types of eczema, some wet and some dry. This is usually at least partially an allergic response to either foods or the environment (animal hair, dust mites found in the home, pollen, polluted air) or both. Inherited allergies (which you may not even be aware of) may also play a part. Low stomach acid has been associated with both eczema and food allergies.

The skin acts as a barrier against bacteria entering the body and also regulates the body's temperature. Babies with under-functioning immune systems are susceptible to this uncomfortable complaint, as well as difficulties in regulating their body temperatures. It is often found in the creases of the arms and legs.

what you can do

If you are breastfeeding and know of any food allergies in either parents or your families, cut them out of your diet. Common food allergens are dairy products, wheat and animal fats.

Some foods are thought to help, so if you are breastfeeding you could try increasing the consumption of essential fatty acids found in tuna, sardines, salmon or anchovies. Oats have been found to contain anti-inflammatory properties and aloe vera is another popular dietary aid.

Vacuum frequently to get rid of dust mites and restrict pets to those rooms with few soft furnishings, such as the kitchen.

Dress your baby in natural, non-irritating, absorbent materials such as cotton. Look for baggy styles with seams that will not rub the affected areas.

HERBAL HELP

One of the easiest ways to give your baby herbal help is through your breastmilk. Before a feed, you can drink herbal teas or recommended alcohol-free tinctures. It is estimated that the herbs consumed will reach the milk supply in approximately 15–30 minutes, and residues may last for up to 48 hours or even longer.

USE NATURAL FIBRES

The skin contains many special nerve endings associated with the sensation of touch, pressure, pain, warmth and cold. If your baby's skin is sensitive, dress her in natural fibres that will allow her skin to breathe easily. Remember that she has no way of regulating her own temperature, so use several light cotton wraps that can be easily removed, or a soft blanket made of natural fibres, as all synthetic garments will make your baby hotter.

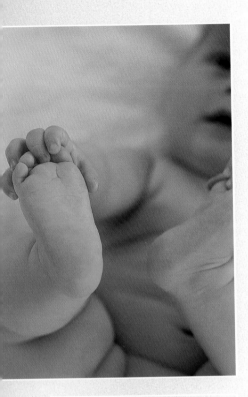

Above *Reflexology may be particularly helpful for skin irritations where the irritated area cannot be massaged itself.*

SPOTS AND BIRTHMARKS

Don't worry if you see small white spots on your baby's skin over the bridge of the nose. These are called milia and are caused by a temporary blockage of the sweat glands. They will disappear in a few days.

A common birthmark, sometimes called a strawberry mark, can become apparent on your baby's skin a few days after birth. This mark gradually disappears over time, and should have faded completely before his third birthday.

complementary therapies that can help

- **Herbal medicine:** consultation. Massage with aloe vera can soothe discomfort. Burdock, chickweed or comfrey ointments can be rubbed into the affected areas, and 2–4 cupfuls of tea made from echinacea, burdock root, gotu kola, comfrey, nettle leaves, lavender flowers, chicory root and artichoke leaves can be added to your baby's bath.
- **Homoeopathy:** consultation. There are lots of different treatments depending on the state of the skin and the cause of the problem.
- **Reflexology:** consultation. If your baby's skin is irritated, or has small fluid-filled blisters, massaging the feet is obviously preferable to body massage. By covering the lymphatic system, reflexology can help the body to eliminate toxins. With skin problems there may be a flare-up for a couple of days after treatment and possibly prior to improvement. This should not be a source of concern.

nappy rash

Nappy rash is a common condition, occuring when a baby's bottom is sealed for a time in a wet nappy. It is caused when ammonia is produced as a result of the reaction between urine and bacteria in the faeces.

what you can do

Let your baby have his nappy off as much as possible. Use warm water and cotton wool to thoroughly clean the area at each nappy change, and avoid the use of petroleum-based products such as mineral oil.

complementary therapies that can help

- **Aromatherapy:** Add 1 drop of lavender or rose essential oil to your baby's bath, then make sure he is dried well. Add 1 drop of either lavender or Roman chamomile essential oil to 2 dessertspoons of zinc and castor oil cream and apply to the rash.

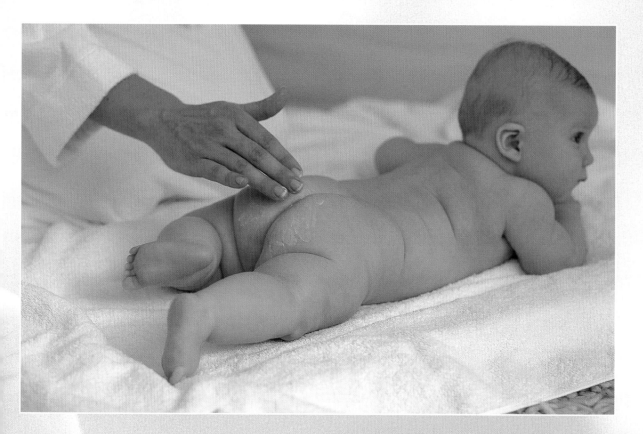

- **Herbal medicine:** consultation. Calendula cream can be helpful. You can also apply a chamomile tea to the rash to reduce acidity and use a light dusting of slippery elm powder or finely ground calendula.
- **Homoeopathy:** consultation. Rhus Tox. or Sulphur are suitable for a scaly red rash.

Above Aloe vera gel has a very good skin healing reaction, as well as being soothing and cooling.

thrush

Thrush is a yeast infection and is most common in babies under 12 months. Babies can get white spots anywhere on their body, but particularly around their mouth and on their tongue (oral thrush). You may also have candida, which is usually dietary related and can be treated with herbs.

what you can do

Wash the area several times a day with raspberry leaf or black walnut tea.

complementary therapies that can help

- **Herbal medicine:** consultation. Special baby acidophilus can help.

teething

Your baby's teeth will probably begin to cut through the gums at around six or seven months – although some babies do not get their first teeth until one year – but they won't all be through until the age of about two or three. When teething, your baby's mood can change, so a cherub can turn into a cranky handful overnight.

HELP WHEN TEETHING

A herbalist can help a baby when they get a rash, vomit or become irritable due to teething, by making up a herbal calcium tea, as calcium is often what they are low in. You can also massage their fingers and toes to aid pain relief and lymphatic drainage.

Some teeth are cut without any pain at all, while others will cause your baby notable discomfort. You may find your child changes from delightful to fretful when she starts teething. When a tooth is coming you may notice a flushed cheek or a red, sore gum area. Your baby will probably dribble and chew on anything she can get her hands on, and pull on her ear lobe.

what you can do

Give your baby something hard to chew on, such as a teething ring, to soothe her gums, provided you are always in attendance to prevent choking. Do not give her anything sweetened to suck on, since sugar can cause tooth decay, even in babies with few teeth.

1 *Using the fingertips of both hands, massage in tiny circles from her temples to her jaw. Do not apply any pressure, simply slide the fingers over her skin. Massage in tiny light circles along her jaw and gently palpate.*

2 *Gently finger stroke from her ear down her neck, encouraging the lymphatics to drain. Repeat on the other side.*

complementary therapies that can help

- **Aromatherapy:** massage the ears (see below) with a mix of 1 drop Roman chamomile and 1 drop lavender essential oils in 30 ml carrier oil.
- **Herbal medicine:** consultation. A catnip and fennel tincture can be massaged into the gums.
- **Homoeopathy:** consultation. Chamomilla teething granules are also available from health-food and complementary therapy shops.
- **Reflexology:** consultation. Working on the toes can help alleviate the pain of teething.

Above Keep teething rings in the fridge so that they are cooling on hot, inflamed gums.

massage for the teething baby

In acupuncture terms, the ear represents the whole of the body and holds 400 acupuncture points. The jaw point is on the ear lobe, the place that babies often naturally try to touch when teething. Touching this acupuncture point on the ear lobe allows your baby's own natural painkillers to be released, so massaging here is a great idea. Warm your hands and smooth in some oil. Look into your baby's eyes and talk lovingly to her throughout this massage routine.

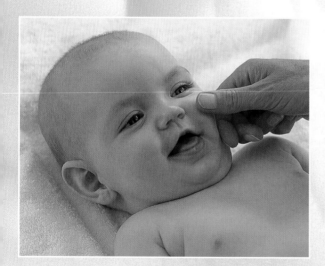

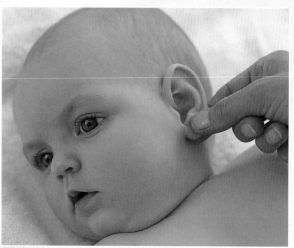

3 *Thumb stroke from the side of her nose down towards her jaw, gently circling on her jaw, again to help the lymph to drain, and to encourage circulation. Repeat on the other side of the nose.*

4 *Massage the back and front of her ear with your thumb and forefinger, following the shape of the ear. Gently squeeze the ear, but do not pinch it, this is a delicate movement. Repeat on the second ear.*

respiratory problems

Breathing problems due to colds or asthma obviously cause great distress to both baby and mother, but there are certain ways that you can help to alleviate discomfort in your child. While crying does allow more oxygen into the lungs, it also creates a very distressed, hot and upset baby.

Above *A number of alternative therapies can halp alleviate the breathing problems associated with a cold.*

colds and coughs

Babies are prone to catching colds and coughs and while you can't cure the common cold, you can help your baby to breathe more easily.

what you can do

Massaging and tapping over your baby's chest and back will help (see pages 89 and 98). You can also try stroking his face down towards the jaw and the sides of his neck, and massaging from the neck to the armpit.

complementary therapies that can help

• **Aromatherapy:** Place 1 drop each of eucalyptus, tea tree and lavender essential oils in 600 ml (1 pint) of steaming water in a bowl. Position this on the floor in a corner of the nursery while your baby is asleep. You can make a room spray by adding 3 drops of eucalyptus essential oil to a plant spray and filling it with water. Spray around the room, but not close to your baby.

• **Herbal medicine:** consultation. Echinacea, thyme, tea tree, wild cherry or lemon balm can all be taken in a tea.

• **Homoeopathy:** consultation. Aconite for a dry cough and croup; Arsenicum for watery nasal discharge, sometimes with wheezing; Belladonna for a feverish cold; Ipecac for coughing accompanied by phlegm or vomiting; Pulsatilla when symptoms are worse in the evening and when lying down, accompanied by catarrh; and Rumex for a constant cough.

• **Reflexology:** consultation. Working across the sinus points will help to unblock a runny nose, although it may become even runnier before it clears.

fever

If your baby has a fever and is crying a lot more than normal then consult your doctor. He may also be off his food as it will be more difficult for him to breathe and feed. It is essential to keep a feverish baby's fluid intake high and to keep him cool.

Above A feverish baby should be seen by a doctor. Small babies become dehydrated quickly so it is important to keep up their fluid intake.

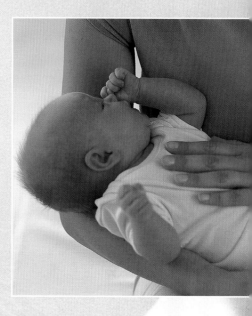

asthma

Asthma is thought by many to be an allergic response to any one of a number of stimuli, including air carried and ingested. It can also be a hereditary condition. The lining of the air passages is very sensitive and an asthma sufferer will respond to allergens with wheezing. Not all babies who wheeze have asthma (and not all babies who have asthma wheeze – they may have a dry, night-time cough instead). Once asthmatic babies grow older and their bronchial tubes widen they will find it easier to breathe. However, if you think your child may be suffering from asthma you should consult your doctor. As your child gets older you may be able to isolate a particular allergen that affects the asthma and therefore try to avoid it.

what you can do

If you are breastfeeding you need to be aware of any food allergies within your family and avoid these foods. Common ingested allergens are cow's milk and dairy products, wheat, yeast, sugar, salt, seafood, caffeine, food additives and aspirin (which should never be given to children).

Asthma can be triggered by common air-carried allergens, such as house dust mites, feathers, pet fur, pollens, moulds, industrial pollutants and cigarette smoke. Vacuum and change the bed sheets often, keep pets restricted to the kitchen and do not smoke around your baby.

complementary therapies that can help

- **Homoeopathy:** consultation. Arsenicum is suitable if your baby is wheezy and restless, especially between 12 midnight and 3am; Camomilla for a sweaty sufferer who is soothed by being carried; Ipecac for coughing that often results in vomiting; and Pulsatilla for the clingy, whiney baby who is worse when lying down.
- **Reflexology:** consultation. Working across the lymphatic and chest points can allow for easier breathing.

HERBAL BATH

Mix together a herbal tea mix of chamomile, catnip, ginger, yarrow and lemon balm. Add the herbal mixture to a baby bath of warm water and gently bathe your baby for five to 10 minutes only. Leave your baby slightly damp and put loose-fitting nightclothes on. Soak a small flannel in a bowl of warm water mixed with 2–3 drops of lavender oil. Wring out and wipe your baby's hands and face regularly to keep them damp. If your baby continues to have a fever then call your doctor.

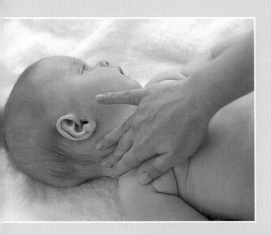

massage for respiratory problems

This is a good massage technique for alleviating the discomfort of minor respiratory problems. Rub some oil into your hands and always look at your baby and talk softly to him as you massage.

1 *Gently stroke down the side of his face then down the side of his neck, flowing on towards his armpits. Aim to sweep rhythmically and continually ten times to help the lymph to clear. You can use both hands at the same time, one on each side of his face, or work one hand and one side at a time.*

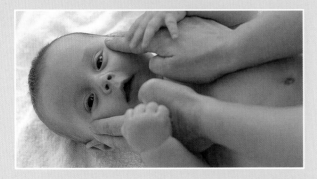

2 *Fingertip massage over his cheeks without using any pressure. Glide the fingers from the edge of his nose to his jaw in one long stroke down the side of his face and neck. Repeat this three times.*

3 *Lightly tap all over his chest and cheeks, then repeat Steps 1 and 2. Follow the lines of his ribs with a soft gentle sweep to the sides of his body. Massage over his chest in circles, from his shoulders towards his last rib.*

4 *Sweep over his eyebrows and circle his temples. Drain down to the neck and armpit.*

5 *Gently squeeze along his fingers and in the web between them. Thumb circle over the top of his hand. This massage relates to the chest and sinuses.*

reflexology massage for respiratory problems

A home reflexology massage may be a good alternative to a body
massage to ease the distress of respiratory blockages.

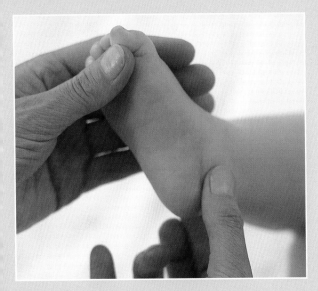

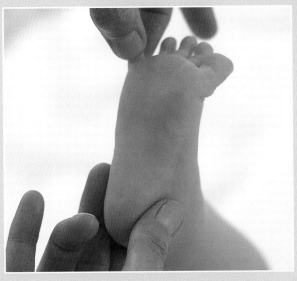

1 *Massage in little circles where his toes meet the sole
of his foot, from his little toe to his big toe and back
several times.*

2 *Give each toe a slight squeeze. You can sing a
nursery rhyme at the same time and make it into
a game if you wish.*

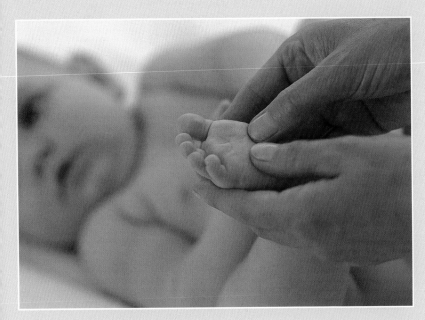

3 *Massage the balls of his feet,
then tap over the top of his feet
lightly and thumb stroke from his
ankles to his toes.*

other common ailments

Here is a look at some of the other common problems – including eye inflammations, earache, disturbed sleep, burns and insect bites or stings – that babies often suffer from. All of these may be helped by complementary therapies, and we will show you how to alleviate the distress of your baby's symptoms.

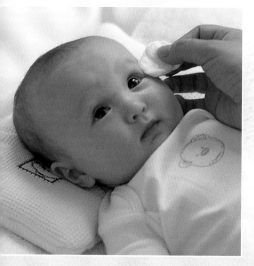

Above *Regular cleaning with cotton wool and sterilized warm saline water will soothe many minor eye problems.*

eye inflammations

Eye inflammations of the outer eye can be bacterial, viral or due to an allergy. If there is no discharge it is usually caused by an allergy or hayfever. If there is a discharge it is usually thick and can glue up your baby's eyes. Not all eye inflammations are conjunctivitus, which is highly contagious.

what you can do

A general eye inflammation, common in newborns, simply requires regular cleaning with cotton wool and sterilized, warm, slightly salty water. Wash your hands thoroughly and sweep the wet cotton wool inwards from the cheek to the inside eye, and change the cotton wool after each sweep, to avoid reinfection. Dry each eye separately with different, dry cotton wall balls.

complementary therapies that can help

• **Herbal medicine:** consultation. For conjunctivitis a golden seal tea or tincture, or chamomile, eyebright and raspberry leaf tea may be prescribed. You can add 1–2 drops of the tincture to an eyebath of boiled and cooled filtered water and bathe the eyes with the mixture.

• **Homoeopathy:** consultation. Aconite is suitable for an injured eye or if a foreign body is present; Belladonna for an itchy inflammation that gets worse with bright light; Euphrasia for itchy, watery or sticky eyes; and Pulsatilla for eyes that are sticky with discharge and itchy, or for blocked tear ducts.

earache

Earaches are often caused by a build-up of fluid in the middle ear, which can lead to an infection and a high temperature.

what you can do

Constant ear infections can be caused by food allergies, but they are usually caused by a viral infection. Gently wash the earlobe and check

Above *Sticky discharge from the eye requires medical attention.*

your child's temperature. Also try not to get your child's head wet. Many children will get over an ear infection themselves without any need for further treatment.

complementary therapies that can help

- **Herbal medicine:** consultation. Warm up lavender essential oil, garlic or mullein oil by standing the bottle in a cup of hot water. Pour 3–5 drops onto cotton wool and use it to plug the ear. Replace the plug twice daily until the infection clears.
- **Homoeopathy:** consultation. Aconite is suitable for a sudden onset ear infection that is worse around midnight or after exposure to the cold; Belladonna for earache accompanied by fever, if the face or ear looks red, and if the right ear is often worse; Chamomilla for a screaming baby who is better for being carried, often when teething; Hepar Sulph. for the onset of earache after or during a cold with catarrh, with or without discharge; and Pulsatilla for a clingy baby who likes to be cuddled and is prone to catarrh.
- **Reflexology:** consultation. The reflexologist can help by clearing infections and catarrhal build-up. You can also try massaging over the toes yourself and massaging the lymphatic points.

KINESIOLOGY

Earache can be caused by food allergies, for example to cow's milk, so try alternative foods, such as goat's milk, instead.

One of the best natural methods to find out your baby's food intolerances is through a consultation with a kinesiologist, who uses muscle testing as their main tool. By surrogate testing you can be muscle tested on behalf of your baby, as it is possible to reflect the imbalances of another person while you are in contact with their skin.

Above If your baby wakes up in the night and will not go back to sleep, check that she is not too hot by holding your hand against the back of her neck.

not sleeping

Babies who don't sleep and are anxious and fretting may be overstimulated, in pain or simply too hot.

complementary therapies that can help

● **Aromatherapy:** Lavender or Roman chamomile essential oils work wonders here. To infuse your baby's nursery with a relaxing scent that will soothe him off to sleep, add 1 drop of lavender or Roman chamomile essential oil to 600 ml (1 pint) of steaming water in a bowl. Place the bowl on the floor, never close to your baby's head, and the steam will circulate the scent around the nursery. The same principle applies to a room spray. In a diffuser add 1 drop of essential oil to 1 dessertspoon of water. A single drop of either essential oil, diluted in a little milk, can be added to a bath.

● **Craniosacral therapy:** consultation. Constant crying could be due to tension held anywhere in the body. An inability to lie in certain positions for long periods of time could be due to tension in the neck.

● **Herbal medicine:** consultation. Chamomile tea may be prescribed.

● **Homoeopathy:** consultation. Bryonia is suitable for the baby that cries a lot while Calcerea Carb. is good for bad dreams.

burns

Despite your best efforts, it is not unheard of for a baby or child to burn himself on a radiator or hot tap.

what you can do

Burns are very shocking so give lots of comfort. Cool the affected area under running cold water or in a cool bath, making sure he is not getting too cold all over. Leave a minor burn to heal itself. If you think it needs to be covered to stop your child from picking at it, use some clean gauze.

If severely burned, take him to hospital for immediate treatment.

complementary therapies that can help

- **Herbal medicine:** consultation. Apply an aloe vera or comfrey paste.
- **Homoeopathy:** consultation. Cream containing hypericum and urtica.

insect bites and stings

Your child will be very upset if he gets stung by a bee or wasp, and insect bites can be particularly irritating.

what you can do

If you can see it, try to remove the sting with tweezers. Do not try to squeeze it out since this may spread the irritating chemical on the end of the sting deeper into the skin. Bee stings can be neutralized by alkaline substances such as bicarbonate of soda; wasp stings can be neutralized with lemon juice or vinegar. If your child has been stung inside the mouth then this can cause breathing problems and requires immediate medical attention.

complementary therapies that can help

- **Herbal medicine:** consultation. Crushed lilac, walnut or elderberry leaves.
- **Homoeopathy:** consultation. Arnica for shock; apis for bee and wasp stings, or any bite that is red, swollen or inflamed; hypericum where there is an infection or sensitive site; ledum for lingering bites that discolour; or urtica urens for itchy red rashes that blister.

Above Not sleeping can be caused by a number of things in small babies – including overstimulation, pain, or something as simple as a blocked nose.

index

acknowledgements

hamlyn acknowledgements

Executive Editor Jane McIntosh
Editor Kate Tucket
Executive Art Editor Karen Sawyer
Designer Janis Utton
Photographer Russell Sadur
Stylist Liz Hippisley
Production Controller Manjit Sihra
Picture Researcher Jennifer Veall

Hamlyn would very much like to thank the following
for the loan of props for photography:

www.modernbaby.co.uk
00 44 (0)800 093 1500

www.jojomamanbebe.co.uk
00 44 (0)20 7924 6844

www.bloomingmarvellous.co.uk
00 44 (0)20 7371 0500

Many thanks also to all the babies and parents who
participated in the photoshoot for their time, energy,
patience and co-operation.

picture acknowledgements

Special Photography
©Octopus Publishing Group Limited/Russell Sadur

Other Photography
Corbis UK Ltd/Owen Franken 15 top right/Rob Lewine
16 centre left
Digital Vision/8-9, 10-11, 12-13, 14-15, 18-19, 19 top,
20-21, 22-23, 28-29, 30-31, 32-33, 34-35, 36-37, 40-41,
46-47, 48-49, 50-51, 52-53, 54-55, 60-61, 62-63, 64-65,
70-71, 74-75, 76-77, 80-81, 82-83, 84-85, 104-105, 106
background, 110-111, 112-113, 114-115, 116-117,
118-119, 122, 125
Getty Images/David Atkinson 33
Octopus Publishing Group Limited/Colin Bowling 69
top left/Gareth Sambidge 118 centre left/Richard Truscott
66-67, 81 top left/Ian Wallace 51 top left, 72-73
Homebase 50 centre left